America's Great Cities

EXPLORE AMERICA

America's Great Cities

Reader's
Digest

THE READER'S DIGEST ASSOCIATION, INC.
Pleasantville, New York / Montreal

AMERICA'S GREAT CITIES was created and produced by ST. REMY MULTIMEDIA INC.

STAFF FOR AMERICA'S GREAT CITIES
Series Editor: Elizabeth Cameron
Art Director: Solange Laberge
Editor: E. W. Lewis
Assistant Editor: Neale McDevitt
Photo Researcher: Linda Castle
Cartography: Hélène Dion, David Widgington
Designer: Anne-Marie Lemay
Research Editor: Robert B. Ronald
Copy Editor: Joan Page McKenna
Contributing Researcher: Olga Dzatko
Index: Linda Cardella Cournoyer
Production Coordinator: Dominique Gagné
Systems Director: Edward Renaud
Technical Support: Mathieu Raymond-Beaubien, Jean Sirois
Scanner Operators: Martin Francoeur, Sara Grynspan

ST. REMY STAFF
PRESIDENT, CHIEF EXECUTIVE OFFICER: Fernand Lecoq
PRESIDENT, CHIEF OPERATING OFFICER: Pierre Léveillé
VICE PRESIDENT, FINANCE: Natalie Watanabe
MANAGING EDITOR: Carolyn Jackson
MANAGING ART DIRECTOR: Diane Denoncourt
PRODUCTION MANAGER: Michelle Turbide

Writers: Jay Clarke—Greater Miami
Jim Henderson—Atlanta
Rose Houk—Santa Fe
Linda Kay—Chicago
K. M. Kostyal—San Francisco
Steven Krolak—Los Angeles, Seattle
Randall Peffer—Boston
Jeremy Schmidt—Salt Lake City
David Yeadon—Manhattan

Contributing Writers: Adriana Barton, Alfred LeMaitre

Address any comments about *America's Great Cities* to U.S. Editor, General Books, c/o Customer Service, Reader's Digest, Pleasantville, NY 10570

READER'S DIGEST STAFF
Senior Editor: Fred DuBose
Editors: Kathryn Bonomi, Susan Bronson
Art Editors: Martha Grossman, Eleanor Kostyk
Production Supervisor: Mike Gallo
Editorial Assistant: Mary Jo McLean

READER'S DIGEST GENERAL BOOKS
Editor-in-Chief, Books and Home
Entertainment: Barbara J. Morgan
Editor, U.S. General Books: David Palmer
Executive Editor: Gayla Visalli
Managing Editor: Christopher Cavanaugh

Opening photographs
Cover: Atlanta skyline, Georgia
Back Cover: Mural on Women's Center, San Francisco, California
Page 2: Palace of Fine Arts, San Francisco, California
Page 5: University of Washington, Seattle, Washington

The credits and acknowledgments that appear on page 144 are hereby made a part of this copyright page.

Library of Congress Cataloging in Publication Data

America's great cities.
        p.   cm.—(Explore America)
    Includes index.
    ISBN 0-7621-0051-6
    1. United States—Guidebooks.   2. United States—History, Local.
3. Cities and towns—United States—Guidebooks   I. Reader's Digest
Association.   II. Series.
    E158.A583   1998
    917.304'929—dc21   97-45579

CONTENTS

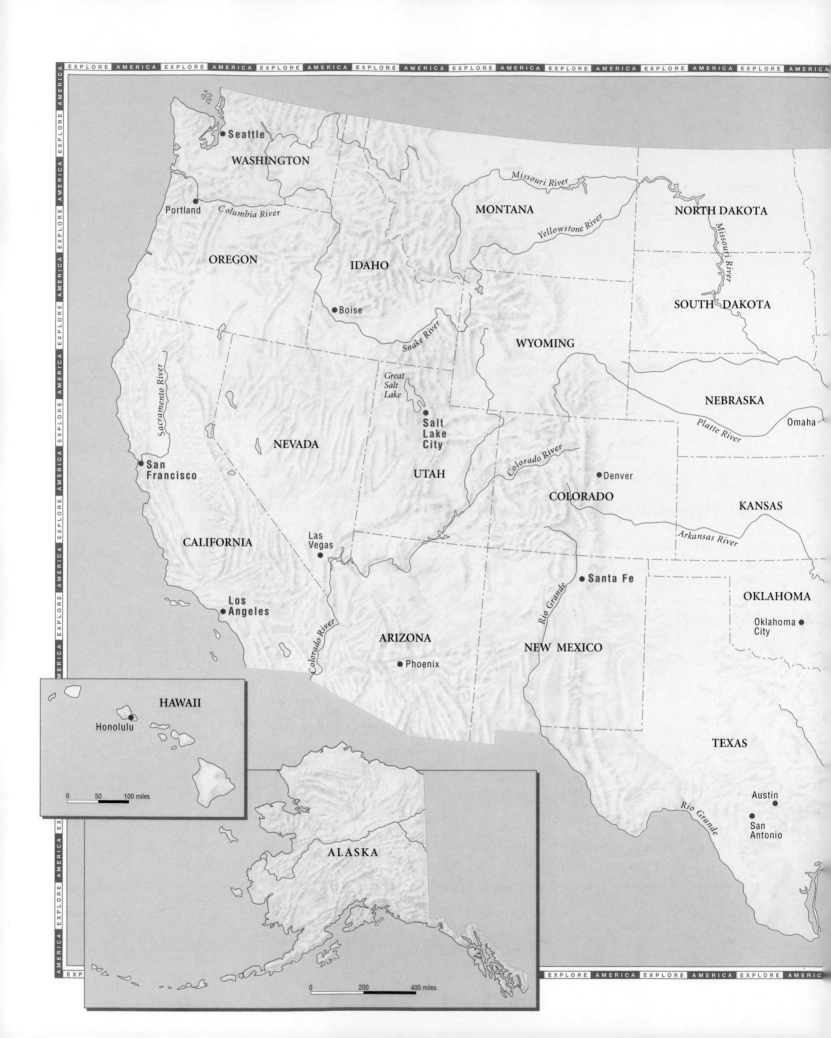

Seattle

WASHINGTON

Portland

Columbia River

OREGON

MONTANA

Missouri River

NORTH DAKOTA

Yellowstone River

Missouri River

IDAHO

Boise

SOUTH DAKOTA

Snake River

WYOMING

Sacramento River

Great
Salt
Lake

NEVADA

Salt
Lake
City

NEBRASKA

Platte River

Omaha

San
Francisco

UTAH

Colorado River

Denver

COLORADO

KANSAS

CALIFORNIA

Las
Vegas

Arkansas River

Los
Angeles

Santa Fe

OKLAHOMA

Colorado River

ARIZONA

Rio Grande

NEW MEXICO

Oklahoma
City

Phoenix

HAWAII

Honolulu

0   50   100 miles

TEXAS

Austin

Rio Grande

San
Antonio

ALASKA

0   200   400 miles

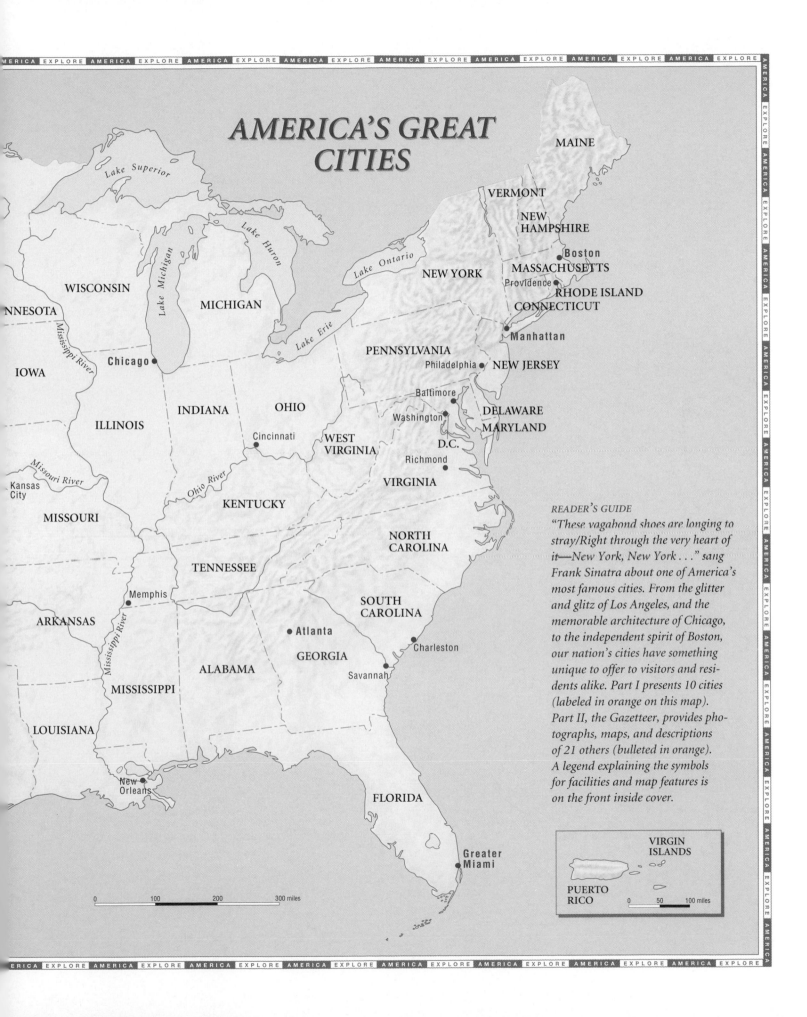

AMERICA'S GREAT CITIES

MAINE

VERMONT

NEW HAMPSHIRE

Lake Superior

Lake Huron

Lake Michigan

Lake Ontario

NEW YORK

Boston

MASSACHUSETTS

Providence

RHODE ISLAND

CONNECTICUT

WISCONSIN

MICHIGAN

MINNESOTA

Mississippi River

Chicago

IOWA

Lake Erie

PENNSYLVANIA

Manhattan

Philadelphia

NEW JERSEY

INDIANA

OHIO

Baltimore

DELAWARE

ILLINOIS

Washington

MARYLAND

Cincinnati

WEST VIRGINIA

D.C.

Missouri River

Kansas City

Ohio River

Richmond

MISSOURI

KENTUCKY

VIRGINIA

NORTH CAROLINA

TENNESSEE

Memphis

SOUTH CAROLINA

ARKANSAS

Mississippi River

Atlanta

Charleston

GEORGIA

ALABAMA

Savannah

MISSISSIPPI

LOUISIANA

New Orleans

FLORIDA

Greater Miami

READER'S GUIDE

"These vagabond shoes are longing to stray/Right through the very heart of it—New York, New York . . ." sang Frank Sinatra about one of America's most famous cities. From the glitter and glitz of Los Angeles, and the memorable architecture of Chicago, to the independent spirit of Boston, our nation's cities have something unique to offer to visitors and residents alike. Part I presents 10 cities (labeled in orange on this map). Part II, the Gazetteer, provides photographs, maps, and descriptions of 21 others (bulleted in orange). A legend explaining the symbols for facilities and map features is on the front inside cover.

0   100   200   300 miles

VIRGIN ISLANDS

PUERTO RICO

0   50   100 miles

BOSTON

*Past and present stand side by side
in this city of brick town houses
and soaring skyscrapers.*

I n 1630, when John Winthrop and his band of
Puritan colonists first saw the verdant slopes of
Beacon Hill, the Shawmut Peninsula bore little
resemblance to what it looks like today. Back then
the peninsula was connected to the mainland by
a narrow strip of land called the Neck. Back Bay
was a soggy area of tidal flats and marshlands.
Three peaks, known as the Trimountaine by the
Puritans, ridged Shawmut's broadest part. Fishing,
then shipping, fed the city's growth, and soon the
shoreline was serrated with wharves. In time,
landfill was added to the shallow waters between
the wharves and the landscape began to assume
its present-day contours. The most dramatic
changes were triggered by the boatloads of
European immigrants—spearheaded by Irish
fleeing the 1845–50 potato famine—arriving at
Boston's harbor. To appease its new citizens'
hunger for land, the city's hills were trimmed and
more than 450 acres of landfill were added to the
peninsula's original 783 acres.

The Back Bay district was one of the earliest
to be created by landfill. It began to take shape
in 1857 when the city trucked in fill from the

FEDERAL ELEGANCE

Federal-style town houses line the brick sidewalks of Beacon Hill's Acorn Street, above, where old-fashioned gas lamps still light pedestrians' way at night.

FAMILY TRADITION

Overleaf: The Public Garden's Swan Boats, which can be rented for a ride on the lagoon, have been operated by the Paget family since 1877. The garden, laid out by Boston landscape architect George F. Meacham in 1837, was the country's first botanical garden.

town of Needham and dumped it in the bay, which had become a rank swampland overflowing with effluent from the city's sewage. As the new district rose, citizens saw it as an opportunity to improve their city. Homes and businesses sprang up as quickly as new land was created, with large areas reserved for public parks. The building of numerous schools and churches added the finishing touches, and by the turn of the century Back Bay was not only filled in, but was also transformed into the setting of an elegant residential district where Boston's merchant princes could feel right at home. On Beacon Street, a well-to-do businessman named John Gardiner Gibson built a five-story mansion in 1860. Today visitors can tour the house, which has been turned into a museum with displays of period furnishings of the Victorian era.

PEOPLE'S PARK

Commonwealth Avenue, or Comm Ave., as Bostonians refer to their grandest boulevard, runs along the length of Back Bay. Its tree-lined mall reflects the design esthetic of the famed French town planner Baron Georges-Eugène Haussmann, who had introduced wide boulevards to the city of Paris, France. At the eastern end of the avenue lies the Public Garden. In

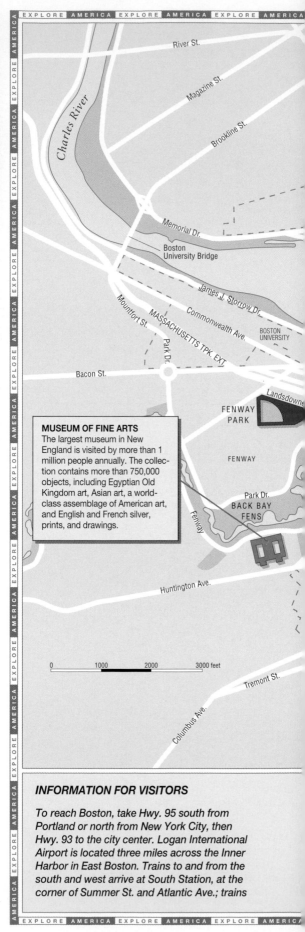

MUSEUM OF FINE ARTS
The largest museum in New England is visited by more than 1 million people annually. The collection contains more than 750,000 objects, including Egyptian Old Kingdom art, Asian art, a world-class assemblage of American art, and English and French silver, prints, and drawings.

0   1000   2000   3000 feet

INFORMATION FOR VISITORS

To reach Boston, take Hwy. 95 south from Portland or north from New York City, then Hwy. 93 to the city center. Logan International Airport is located three miles across the Inner Harbor in East Boston. Trains to and from the south and west arrive at South Station, at the corner of Summer St. and Atlantic Ave.; trains

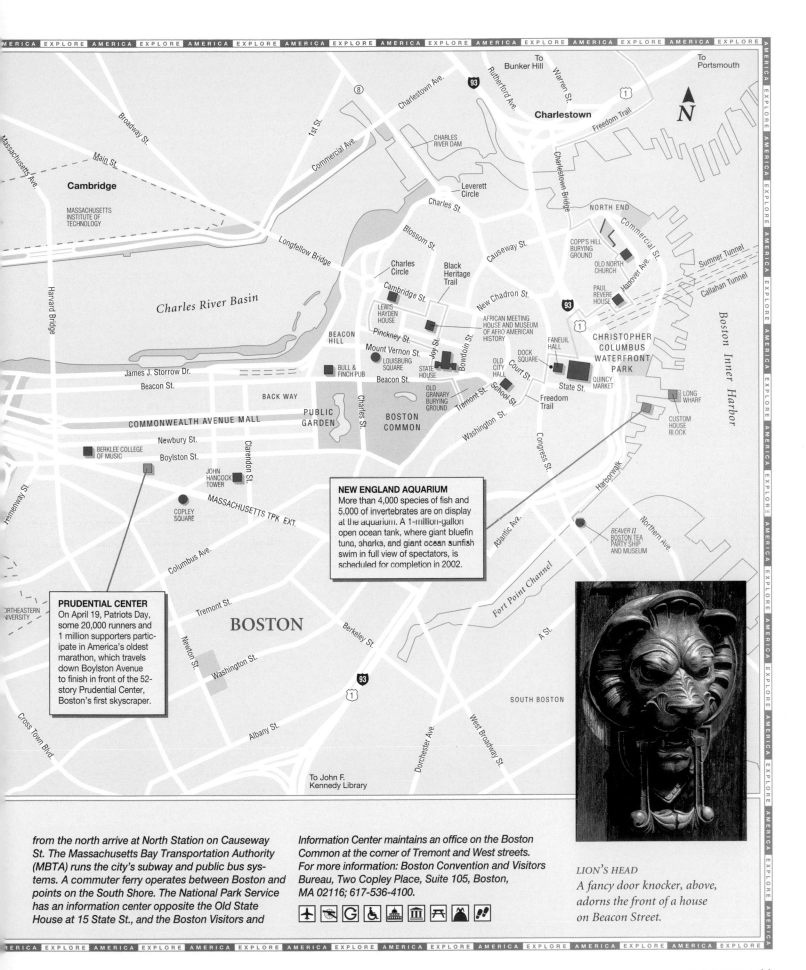

To Bunker Hill

To Portsmouth

Charlestown

Charlestown Ave.

Rutherford Ave.

Warren St.

Charlestown Bridge

Freedom Trail

1st St.

Commercial Ave.

CHARLES RIVER DAM

Leverett Circle

Charles St.

Blossom St.

Causeway St.

NORTH END

Commercial St.

COPP'S HILL BURYING GROUND

OLD NORTH CHURCH

PAUL REVERE HOUSE

Hanover Ave.

Sumner Tunnel

Callahan Tunnel

Cambridge

MASSACHUSETTS INSTITUTE OF TECHNOLOGY

Broadway St.

Main St.

Massachusetts Ave.

Longfellow Bridge

Charles Circle

Cambridge St.

LEWIS HAYDEN HOUSE

Black Heritage Trail

New Chardon St.

AFRICAN MEETING HOUSE AND MUSEUM OF AFRO AMERICAN HISTORY

FANEUIL HALL

CHRISTOPHER COLUMBUS WATERFRONT PARK

Boston Inner Harbor

Harvard Bridge

Charles River Basin

BEACON HILL

Pinckney St.

Mount Vernon St.

LOUISBURG SQUARE

BULL & FINCH PUB

Joy St.

Bowdoin St.

STATE HOUSE

DOCK SQUARE

OLD CITY HALL

Court St.

State St.

QUINCY MARKET

James J. Storrow Dr.

Beacon St.

BACK WAY

Charles St.

PUBLIC GARDEN

BOSTON COMMON

Beacon St.

OLD GRANARY BURYING GROUND

Tremont St.

School St.

Freedom Trail

Washington St.

LONG WHARF

CUSTOM HOUSE BLOCK

COMMONWEALTH AVENUE MALL

Newbury St.

BERKLEE COLLEGE OF MUSIC

Boylston St.

JOHN HANCOCK TOWER

Clarendon St.

MASSACHUSETTS TPK EXT.

COPLEY SQUARE

Congress St.

Atlantic Ave.

Harborwalk

Northern Ave.

BEAVER II BOSTON TEA PARTY SHIP AND MUSEUM

NEW ENGLAND AQUARIUM
More than 4,000 species of fish and 5,000 of invertebrates are on display at the aquarium. A 1-million-gallon open ocean tank, where giant bluefin tuna, sharks, and giant ocean sunfish swim in full view of spectators, is scheduled for completion in 2002.

PRUDENTIAL CENTER
On April 19, Patriots Day, some 20,000 runners and 1 million supporters participate in America's oldest marathon, which travels down Boylston Avenue to finish in front of the 52-story Prudential Center, Boston's first skyscraper.

NORTHEASTERN UNIVERSITY

Columbus Ave.

Tremont St.

Newton St.

Washington St.

BOSTON

Berkeley St.

Fort Point Channel

A St.

SOUTH BOSTON

West Broadway St.

Dorchester Ave.

Cross Town Blvd.

Albany St.

To John F. Kennedy Library

LION'S HEAD
A fancy door knocker, above, adorns the front of a house on Beacon Street.

from the north arrive at North Station on Causeway St. The Massachusetts Bay Transportation Authority (MBTA) runs the city's subway and public bus systems. A commuter ferry operates between Boston and points on the South Shore. The National Park Service has an information center opposite the Old State House at 15 State St., and the Boston Visitors and Information Center maintains an office on the Boston Common at the corner of Tremont and West streets. For more information: Boston Convention and Visitors Bureau, Two Copley Place, Suite 105, Boston, MA 02116; 617-536-4100.

AMERICA EXPLORE AMERICA EXPLORE AMERICA EXPLORE AMERICA EXPLORE AMERICA EXPLORE AMERICA EXPLORE AMERICA EXPLORE AMERICA EXPLORE AMERICA EXPLORE

BOSTON 11

SECOND EMPIRE INFLUENCE
Boston's Old City Hall, above, on School Street, was turned into a commercial building in 1968 when the municipal offices were moved to Government Center. The French Second Empire building now houses various businesses and a fine French restaurant.

SIMPLE PLEASURES
Steamed hot dogs satisfy baseball fans at Fenway Park, right, when the Red Sox take to the field. Hall of Fame slugger Babe Ruth made his debut in this arena in 1914— as a pitcher.

May the garden is redolent with the scent of saucer magnolia blossoms. Ranks of red and yellow tulips proudly flaunt their colors. A quaint suspension footbridge crosses a lagoon, offering a perch for watching the water ballet of swans and ducks and the leisurely progression of antique swan boats. Together with the adjacent Boston Common, the garden creates a quiet world away from the hustle and bustle of Boston's busy downtown streets.

PUBLIC PLACES AND GREEN SPACES The Boston Common, a 48-and-a-half-acre green space, has served as Boston's political and social forum since early Colonial days. The Puritans grazed their cattle and sheep here. Less benignly, they executed people accused of being heretics, witches, and adulterers near the Common's Great Elm, which dominated the pasture until the tree was blown down in a gale in 1876. In 1740, when the population of Boston was about 18,000, more than 23,000 people gathered in the Common to listen to a sermon by a charismatic English preacher named George Whitefield. Five years later

Bostonians gathered here to celebrate the fall of the French fortress in Louisbourg, Nova Scotia, a victory achieved through the valiant action of the Massachusetts Militia. One of the two British regiments sent to quell the colonies' revolutionary fervor in the 1770's camped in the Common, and when Chief Black Hawk and his warriors visited Boston during a goodwill tour in 1837, thousands watched them dance on the wide-open space.

The Common is as popular today as it was in the past. On warm days groups of students stroll through the park and picnic on its long expanses of green grass. The city is dotted with some 60 institutions of higher learning and enjoys the invigorating atmosphere of a college campus. One is the Berklee College of Music, the world's largest independent college of music, whose graduates include Quincy Jones, Branford Marsalis, and John Scofield. Two other world-class institutions are situated across the Charles River: the Massachusetts Institute of Technology (MIT) and Harvard University. MIT, which specializes in scientific and technological training, opened in 1866 in a small Back Bay structure named the Rogers Building after its

The lawns outside the State House are the setting for a number of statues, including those of the orator Daniel Webster and two religious dissidents, Puritan Anne Hutchinson and Quaker Mary Dyer. In 1633 Hutchinson and Dyer were banned from Massachusetts for criticizing the narrow interpretations of the ruling Puritan clergy. Hutchinson went on to become one of the founders of Rhode Island. Dyer, however, was eventually hanged in 1660 for her beliefs. A statue of her by American sculptor Sylvia Shaw Judson was dedicated in 1959 and bears Dyer's last words: "My life availeth me not in comparison to the liberty of the truth."

Across the street from the State House stands the Shaw Monument, honoring Col. Robert Gould Shaw and the men of the 54th Massachusetts Regiment for their sacrifice in the Civil War. Although Shaw and his fellow officers were

founder, William Barton Rogers. As its enrollment expanded, the university purchased a 50-acre site across the river in Cambridge, where MIT now keeps company with its equally prestigious neighbor, Harvard University. Founded in 1636 by John Harvard, the son of a butcher from Stratford-on-Avon, England, the university's illustrious alumni include six presidents: John Adams (1755), John Quincy Adams (1787), Rutherford B. Hayes (1845), Theodore Roosevelt (1880), Franklin Roosevelt (1904), and John F. Kennedy (1940).

THE STATE HOUSE

After strolling through the Common, visitors can head over to inspect the golden-domed State House, which overlooks its northeastern corner. Following the Revolutionary War, the commonwealth of Massachusetts commissioned the preeminent architect Charles Bulfinch to design a building for the legislature. He was influenced by the neoclassical work of Scottish architect Robert Adams, and this redbrick building, with its dome and portico of Corinthian columns, reflects Bulfinch's mastery of classical proportions. Paul Revere, as grand master of the Grand Lodge of Masons, assisted in laying the building's cornerstone in 1795 on pastureland that was once part of patriot John Hancock's estate.

white, the regiment's enlisted men were all free African-Americans from Massachusetts who had volunteered to join the Union forces. The troops fought bravely in the 1863 assault on Fort Wagner, South Carolina, and many died in the attack. The carved relief depicting the regiment marching down Beacon Street is considered to be one of Boston's finest pieces of public art. The monument was designed by Augustus Saint-Gaudens and dedicated in 1897; in 1982 the names of the soldiers killed at Fort Wagner were added.

One of the recruiting agents for the 54th Regiment was a free African-American named Lewis Hayden. The house in which Hayden and his wife, Harriet, lived still stands on Phillips Street

OUTDOOR CORNUCOPIA
Haymarket Square in the North End, above, is one of Boston's vibrant outdoor markets. Numerous food stalls display an appetizing selection of fresh fruits and vegetables.

in Beacon Hill. Born in Lexington, Kentucky, Hayden escaped enslavement in 1816 through the Underground Railroad and ended up in Boston, then a haven for runaway slaves. In 1850, when the Fugitive Slave Law granted Southern slave owners the legal right to recapture their slaves, Hayden made his home a vital station on the Underground Railroad. Later, his only son was killed while serving in the Union navy. The Hayden House is closed to the public, but visitors who follow the Black Heritage Trail stop there and at 13 other sites, including the African Meeting House and the Abiel Smith School. The walking trail explores the history of the African-Americans, who lived primarily on the north slope of Beacon Hill in the 19th century.

HOME OF THE BRAHMINS

Beacon Hill is known as the heart of Old Boston. Its 19th-century redbrick town houses, with their decorative bow fronts, colorful window boxes, and painted shutters, recall the days in the mid-19th century when the arbiters of Boston's social and literary world were members of a relatively small group of wealthy New England families known as the Brahmins—a humorous reference to the highest caste of Hindu society. Their numbers included such celebrated writers as Oliver Wendell Holmes and Henry Wadsworth Longfellow.

On snowy evenings before Christmas, groups of carolers wind through the Hill's narrow, twisting cobblestone streets and congregate in Louisburg Square below the wrought-iron balconies of elegant town houses. Sometimes residents send mugs of hot cider down to the caroling celebrants. Later the crowd might walk downhill to the Charles Street emporiums, where the windows are decorated with holiday lights and festive displays, or stop in at the Bull & Finch Pub on Beacon Street, famous as the inspiration for the television comedy *Cheers*.

Before the new State House was built, Beacon Hill was little more than a dense thicket of brambles and blackberry bushes on the edge of the Old Granary Burying Ground. A list of the personages buried here reads like a revolutionary roll call: Samuel Adams, John Hancock, and Paul Revere. The graveyard is also the final resting place of Benjamin Franklin's parents, six Massachusetts state governors, and Crispus Attucks, the first person to be killed in the 1770 Boston Massacre, when British soldiers fired on a mob of angry Bostonians.

The two-and-a-half-mile-long red line that marks the Freedom Trail passes near the Old Granary Burying Ground. In a city famous for its walks, this short trail is one of the best. It begins in the Boston Common at Tremont Street and links together 16 historic sites, ending at the Bunker Hill

Monument in Charlestown. As it makes its way along Boston's crooked streets, the trail winds past Dock Square, between Congress Street and Faneuil Hall. Originally situated beside the sea at the Town Dock, Dock Square is now about a quarter mile from the waterfront. In the 18th century, ships weighed anchor here and unloaded their goods.

Dock Square was recommended as the perfect site for a marketplace, but the idea was opposed by local merchants and farmers—even after a wealthy local businessman named Peter Faneuil offered to put up the money to build it. Despite the controversy, Faneuil Hall was erected in 1740, with the painter John Smibert serving as its architect. A gold-plated grasshopper, a 17th-century symbol of prosperity, was installed as a weather vane on the hall's central turret. The market was gutted by fire in 1761, but was quickly rebuilt. Produce and other goods were sold on the ground floor, while the second floor served as a meeting hall where patriot leaders such as James Otis and Samuel Adams gave fiery speeches during the years leading up to the war with Britain. From 1805 to 1806 Charles Bulfinch expanded Faneuil Hall and

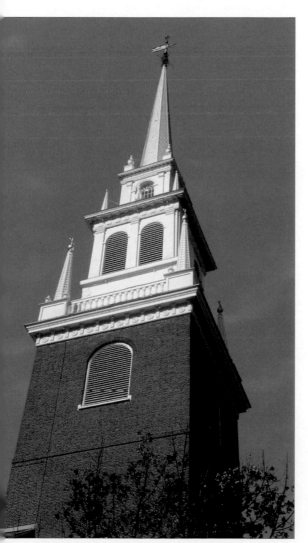

had the original weather vane reinstalled. According to legend, during the War of 1812, anyone who could not identify the insect on the weather vane at Faneuil Hall was believed to be a spy.

Even the expanded hall was insufficient to meet the needs of Boston's rapidly growing population, and in 1825 Mayor Josiah Quincy decided to have another market built. To add to the confusion, the new market is known both as Faneuil Hall Market Place and Quincy Market. In the early 1970's the marketplace and neighboring Faneuil Hall were restored. Today visitors to Quincy Market can walk along the flanking rows of brick and granite warehouses known as the North and South markets, and stop at more than 100 indoor shops and numerous cafés, restaurants, bars, and food stalls. Freshly cut flowers are sold at a market in the pedestrian mall, and benches beneath shady trees offer seating for impromptu performances by a collection of clowns, jugglers, artists, and musicians.

Not long ago Boston Harbor, to the east of the market, was a depressed area. But when Faneuil Hall experienced its renaissance, city planners created the two-mile-long pedestrian Harborwalk, which leads south from the park toward the old wharves and Fort Point Channel and offers splendid views of a yacht basin and the shipping channel. Along the Harborwalk lie Long Wharf and the granite-faced Custom House Block, where Nathaniel Hawthorne worked as a clerk from 1839 to 1841, writing children's fiction on the side. Now the warehouses are used as offices and restaurants, and the wharf serves as a terminal for tour boats.

BOSTON PLEASURES
The glass roof of the Venetian courtyard in the Isabella Stewart Gardner Museum, above, allows sufficient sunlight for plants to bloom year-round. This Back Bay museum houses a collection of masterpieces, including Titian's Europa. *During the night of March 18, 1990, thieves broke into the museum and stole 13 rare art objects, including paintings by Degas, Manet, Rembrandt, and Vermeer. Across town in Boston's North End, the celebrated belfry of Christ Church, left, also known as Old North Church, is another tourist attraction. On the night of April 18, 1775, Robert Newman, the church sexton, hung signal lanterns from the steeple to warn the Minutemen in Charlestown that the British were coming.*

A TALL TALE
A row of tall ships, opposite page, lines the dock in Boston Harbor. Long Wharf, which was constructed in 1710, is almost 2,000 feet long. It dramatically increased the port's docking space.

As Harborwalk crosses the bridge over Fort Point Channel, the *Beaver II,* moored by the Congress Street Bridge, comes into view. Costumed guides on board re-create the Boston Tea Party. The ship is a replica of one of the three vessels overtaken the night of December 16, 1773, by a group of patriots disguised as Indians, who jettisoned the ships' chests of English tea to protest the British import tax.

One of the protesting patriots may have been the silversmith Paul Revere, whose house at No. 19 North Square in Boston's North End is the oldest building in downtown Boston. Paul Revere was 35 years old when he and his family moved into the Tudor-style dwelling in 1770. The Paul Revere Memorial Association, which has restored the 1680 house, maintains a small period garden in the back

where lady's mantle and Johnny-jump-ups continue to flourish as they did in the 18th century.

Boston's North End, at the base of Copp's Hill, is primarily an Italian neighborhood. In Colonial times the neighborhood was often called the Island of North Boston because a creek cut the area off from the peninsula. The quarter was the home of some of the city's wealthiest citizens, many of whom were loyal to the crown. When the British fleet withdrew from the city on March 17, 1776, it car-

their own. Today *caffè* and *ristoranti* beckon visitors to stop and enjoy the atmosphere of the area. Italian men sit in the shade playing checkers in Paul Revere Mall, one end of which is presided over by Cyrus Dallin's sculpture of the beloved patriot.

Visitors strolling through Boston's neighborhoods come face-to-face with the past. It is a city that takes pride in its history, even relishing its nickname of Beantown, which harks back to the days when the Puritans first settled here. Because

SOUTHERN VIEW
The John Hancock Tower dwarfs its neighbors on the southern bank of the Charles River Basin, left. At 60 stories tall and 790 feet high, the John Hancock Tower is the tallest building in New England. It was designed by Henry Cobb of I. M. Pei and Partners and built between 1968 and 1976. Its neighbors are two older buildings that were also once used by the John Hancock Mutual Life Insurance Co.

ried more than a thousand of these Tories on board. Sailors and transients replaced those who left until Irish immigrant families began moving there in the 1820's, followed by waves of other Europeans until, by 1920, Italian-Americans had claimed the North End's twisted byways and small plazas as

their religion forbade them to work on the Sabbath, they began the Saturday night tradition of simmering a pot of baked beans to feed their families the next day. Still renowned for its beans, Boston has grown from its resolute Puritan roots to become the cosmopolitan city it is today.

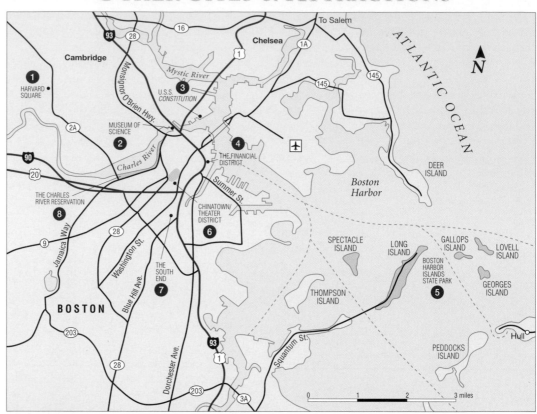

The pediment of Holden Chapel, below, located on the grounds of Harvard University, is adorned with the coat of arms of the Holden family. Fanciful carvings of cherubs surround the coat of arms.

① HARVARD SQUARE

A short subway ride across the Charles River from downtown Boston, Harvard Square stands outside Johnston Gate, one of many gates to Harvard University. The square's bookstores, restaurants, clothing stores, and other shops are crowded with students, faculty, and visitors from the Boston area and beyond. In good weather street performers entertain passersby. Located in Cambridge.

② MUSEUM OF SCIENCE

This world-class museum, housed in a building of glass, brick, and concrete, contains more than 1,000 displays, including the world's largest Van de Graaff generator (capable of producing 15-foot-long lightning bolts) and a life-size replica of a *Tyrannosaurus rex*. Other attractions include the Charles Hayden Planetarium; the Mugar Omni Theater, where films are viewed on huge screens inside a four-story-high dome; and the Live Animal Stage, where visitors can see snakes, ducks, porcupines, and owls up close. Located in Science Park just off the Monsignor O'Brien Hwy.

③ U.S.S. *CONSTITUTION*

This black frigate, whose tall masts tower above Boston's inner harbor, has become a well-known city landmark. Built in 1797 to protect American interests abroad, the U.S.S. *Constitution* distinguished itself in the War of 1812, during which its shellproof oak hull earned the vessel the nickname Old Ironsides. The ship returned to its home port of Boston in 1897 after long and valiant service. The ship has been restored several times, most recently in 1973 in preparation for the nation's bicentennial. The oldest commissioned ship in the United States Navy, the frigate sailed once again in 1997 on the 200th anniversary of its launching. The ship is accessible by water taxi from Rowes Wharf. Located across the Charles River.

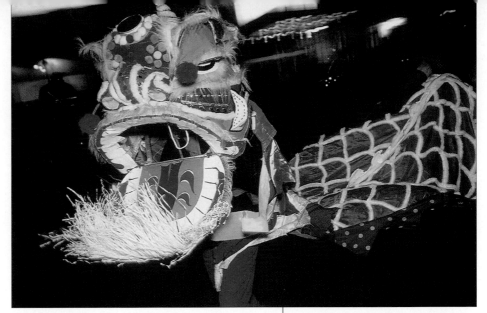

❹ THE FINANCIAL DISTRICT

During the 1980's, glass-and-steel towers sprang up among the historical and cultural attractions in Boston's downtown district. The Old State House dates from 1713 and marks the site of the 1770 Boston Massacre, when British soldiers fired on an angry mob of Bostonians. The Old Corner Bookstore, which now specializes in regional titles, has attracted Boston's literati since 1828. Such famed authors as Henry David Thoreau, Nathaniel Hawthorne, and Ralph Waldo Emerson once purchased their books here. At one time the building served as the offices of the *Boston Globe*. At the busy intersection known as the Downtown Crossing, shoppers can browse through a variety of department stores—among them Filene's, famous for its bargain basement. Nearby Lincoln Filene Park provides a welcome respite from the crowded streets. Located in downtown Boston.

❺ BOSTON HARBOR ISLANDS STATE PARK

Many of the 30 islets in this state park, including Georges, Gallops, Bumkin, Grape, and Slate, are open to the public for hiking, camping, fishing, picnicking, and swimming. Commercial ferryboats transport visitors to Georges Island from Long Wharf, and during the summer there is limited water-taxi service between the islands. Native Americans inhabited the islands as early as 4000 B.C., and Puritans, including Gov. John Winthrop, established farms here in the 17th century. Fort Warren, on Georges Island, served as a prison for Confederate

soldiers during the Civil War. Boston Light, situated on Little Brewster Island, has been a fixture since 1716 and is one of the last manned lighthouses left in the country. The park is located in Boston Harbor.

❻ CHINATOWN/THEATER DISTRICT

Boston's two-block Chinatown is home to thousands of people of Asian heritage and boasts many restaurants and curio shops. The adjacent Theater District contains some of the city's most lavish playhouses, including the Shubert Theater and the Colonial Theater, renowned for its rococo lobby of Pompeian marble and the bronze banister on its staircase. Located south of the Boston Common.

❼ THE SOUTH END

Once a point of entry for immigrants from Ireland, the West Indies, Lebanon, and Central and South America, the South End has become the residence of choice for many of the city's artists, performers, and writers. Today the district's cafés, bistros, and galleries percolate with activity. The neighborhood's redbrick town houses constitute one of the finest restored Victorian row house districts in America. Located south of Herald St.

❽ THE CHARLES RIVER RESERVATION

One of many parks and green spaces in the city, this two-mile-long esplanade offers some of the best urban vistas. Pedestrians, joggers, and inline skaters follow paths along the shores of the Charles River, which is dotted with hundreds of small sailboats and rowing shells in the summer. The Hatch Shell amphitheater has served as a venue for summer concerts since 1940. The Boston Pops has been performing in the reservation since 1929. Hikers can cross the picturesque Storrow Lagoon on a series of stone bridges to see the Lotta Fountain and a memorial to Oliver Wendell Holmes. The walkway begins at the Charles River Dam. A spectacular fireworks display is put on every July 4.

Representatives of the Chinese community of Boston maneuver a dragon, above, during the city's annual First Night Parade. The parade, which is held New Year's Eve, features members of Boston's arts and entertainment groups and its cultural organizations.

The U.S.S. Constitution, *left, is moored in the Charlestown Navy Yard. Launched in 1797, the frigate's final battle was waged in February 1815, off the coast of Africa. When the smoke cleared, the* Constitution *had captured two British ships.*

MANHATTAN

One of New York's five boroughs, Manhattan is renowned for its cultural richness and ethnic diversity.

From its beginnings in 1625 as a Dutch trading enclave called New Amsterdam to the shining metropolis it is today, Manhattan has grown to symbolize America's can-do attitude and determination to let nothing stand in the way of growth, progress, and prosperity. The early waves of immigrants arrived primarily from 1840 to 1925, and since 1886 newcomers have been greeted by the Statue of Liberty, rising 150 feet from her majestic plinth in New York Harbor. Many of them were processed at the immigration center on Ellis Island, the halls of which have been refurbished and are open to the public.

"A map of the city, colored to designate nationalities, would show more stripes than on the skin of a zebra and more colors than any rainbow," claimed Jacob Riis, renowned photographer of immigrants in the early 1900's. "New York isn't a melting pot, it's a boiling pot," enthused Thomas Edmund Dewey, governor of New York State in 1942. The city in the 1940's was expanding northward from the haphazard labyrinth of downtown's narrow lanes into the burgeoning grid of streets and avenues that eventually stretched all the

way to the upper limits of the island. The palaces of the titans of industry and commerce rose in an extravagant variety of architectural styles along Fifth Avenue. The teeming tenements of the Lower East Side, Chinatown, and Little Italy emerged, along with the more decorous enclaves around Washington Square, Gramercy Park, Murray Hill, and the Upper East and West Side neighborhoods. Quaint greens and squares dot the island, and the great 843-acre oasis of Central Park, considered to be one of the world's most beautiful public spaces, still provides harried residents with a place to escape to from the frenzied pace of the city.

A CITY TAKES SHAPE

The island of Manhattan, tightly bounded by the Hudson, East, and Harlem rivers, is 2.5 miles wide and less than 13 miles long, but it encompasses 22.6 square miles of some of the most expensive real estate in the world. Legend has it that the island was bought from Native Americans for 60 Dutch guilders, or about $24, by Gov. Gen. Peter Minuit in 1626. The first permanent settlement took root in lower Manhattan, where the former U.S. Custom House stands across the street from Battery Park. Mercury, the Roman god of commerce, sits atop the 44 Corinthian columns that surround the building; outside, sculptor Daniel Chester French's *The Four Continents* pays homage to the commercial links the city had with Asia, America, Europe, and Africa. A walk along the tree-shaded promenade at Battery Park offers vistas of the great harbor, the Statue of Liberty, and Ellis Island.

A trip aboard the Staten Island Ferry, which departs from Battery Park, is both free and unforgettable. As the ferry pulls away from the island,

sightseers are afforded a sweeping view of the jumble of skyscrapers that make up New York's fabled skyline. As the city expanded, it became apparent that the only direction it could grow was up. The city's shimmering facade of glass-and-steel towers is among the world's most elegant sights. At night the Empire State Building, the Art Deco–style Chrysler Building, the World Trade Center, and other structures become spotlighted treasures.

The World Trade Center, whose 1,360-foot twin towers no longer show marks of the terrorist bombing of 1993, is one of the most distinctive features of Manhattan's dramatic skyline. Some 50,000 people work in this city within a city, which includes a vast underground shopping and restaurant complex. From the enclosed observation deck on the 107th floor of Two World Trade Center, visitors have an unparalleled view of the city. Free summer concerts are held in the five-acre main plaza. An elegant pedestrian overpass leads to the four towers of the World Financial Center and the Winter Garden, both designed by architect Cesar Pelli. The glassed-in atrium of the Winter Garden is as large as the main floor of Grand Central Station. During the winter this enormous conservatory, with its towering 45-foot-high palm trees, evokes the feeling of a more temperate clime.

To appreciate Manhattan's ties to the sea, visitors should head to the South Street Seaport and the Fulton Fish Market. This slice of Old New York is set amid a restoration of 19th-century city waterfront wharves, old warehouses, and cobblestone streets. At the South Street Seaport, visitors can view a four-masted barkentine; a square-rigged, iron-hulled vessel; a steam-powered ferryboat; and a Gloucester fishing schooner that once sold its catch of the day at nearby Fulton Fish Market. Although the fish now come by truck, the market is still a going concern, especially at 4 a.m., when restaurateurs arrive to sort through the seafood at this historic landmark.

To the north of South Street Seaport is the warrenlike neighborhood of Chinatown, home to one of the largest Chinese communities in the Western Hemisphere. The area is centered on Canal and Mott streets, where countless noodle shops and restaurants—some of which cram their windows facing the street with soy-roasted ducks, chickens, and whole crackle-skinned sides of pork—evoke the atmosphere of the Far East.

The adjoining neighborhood of Little Italy, now limited primarily to Mulberry Street, is an enclave of densely packed four- and five-story walk-up tenements built in the late 1800's. Undoubtedly the most popular event here is the two-week-long September Feast of San Gennaro, sponsored by the San Gennaro Church on nearby Baxter Street.

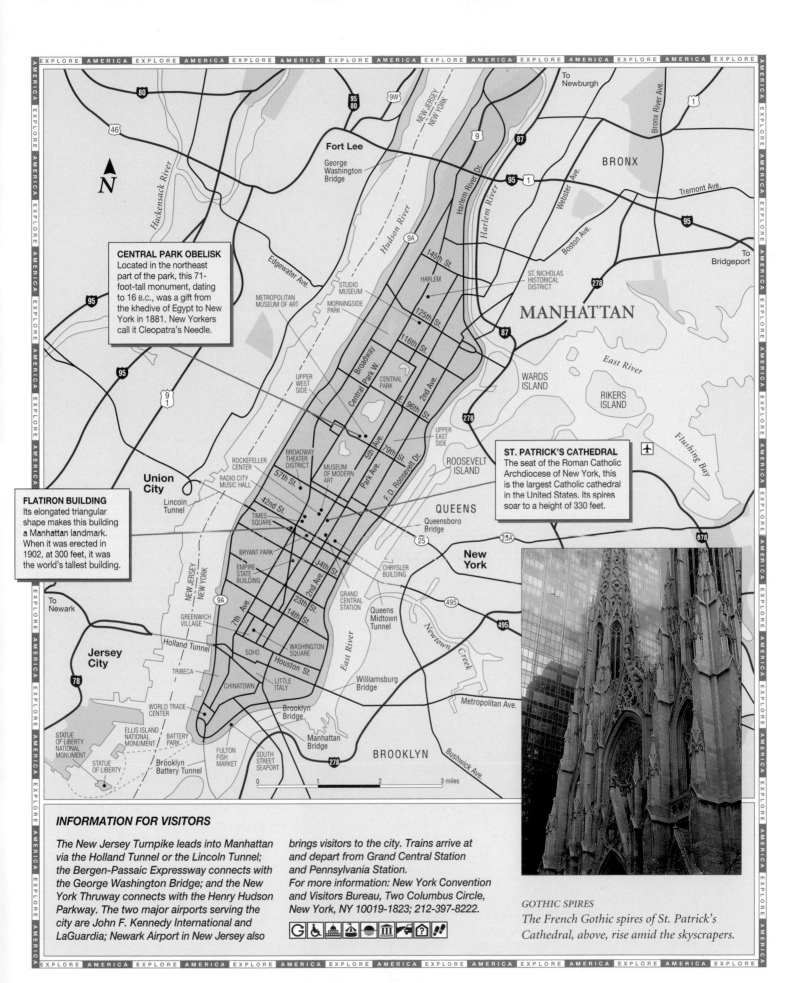

CENTRAL PARK OBELISK
Located in the northeast part of the park, this 71-foot-tall monument, dating to 16 B.C., was a gift from the khedive of Egypt to New York in 1881. New Yorkers call it Cleopatra's Needle.

FLATIRON BUILDING
Its elongated triangular shape makes this building a Manhattan landmark. When it was erected in 1902, at 300 feet, it was the world's tallest building.

ST. PATRICK'S CATHEDRAL
The seat of the Roman Catholic Archdiocese of New York, this is the largest Catholic cathedral in the United States. Its spires soar to a height of 330 feet.

INFORMATION FOR VISITORS

The New Jersey Turnpike leads into Manhattan via the Holland Tunnel or the Lincoln Tunnel; the Bergen-Passaic Expressway connects with the George Washington Bridge; and the New York Thruway connects with the Henry Hudson Parkway. The two major airports serving the city are John F. Kennedy International and LaGuardia; Newark Airport in New Jersey also brings visitors to the city. Trains arrive at and depart from Grand Central Station and Pennsylvania Station.
For more information: New York Convention and Visitors Bureau, Two Columbus Circle, New York, NY 10019-1823; 212-397-8222.

GOTHIC SPIRES
The French Gothic spires of St. Patrick's Cathedral, above, rise amid the skyscrapers.

Mulberry Street is closed to traffic, illuminated tinsel arches span the thoroughfares, and throngs gather to play fairground games and treat themselves to Italian sausage, zeppole, cannoli, and calzone. A similar festival held in June celebrates St. Anthony of Padua. Both festivals serve as reminders of Manhattan's enduring Italian culture.

To the north and west are the newly revived neighborhoods of SoHo and TriBeCa, both acronyms that refer to their location: SoHo is short for South of Houston, and TriBeCa stands for Triangle Below Canal. SoHo reached its nadir in the late 1960's, when 30 or so blocks of worn-out five-story warehouses, sweatshops, and small factories huddled along cobblestone streets were declared a wasteland and became ripe for the wrecker's ball. The amazing diversity and richness of the cast-iron fronted architecture that transforms these structures into elegant neoclassical masterpieces was more or less ignored. Only when New York's legendary city planner Robert Moses set out to build an expressway through the area did the outcries arise and the renaissance of the neighborhood begin. Soon painters, sculptors, and writers began to move into the area. Their lofts and studios were—and still are—often reached by commercial elevators and steep flights of stairs.

Galleries set up shop, the expressway plan was abandoned, and the cast-iron buildings were meticulously restored, particularly around Broadway and along Greene Street. This is the heart of the SoHo Historic District, where 50 structures built between 1869 and 1895 have survived; all display the distinctive exterior classical ornamentation for which the district is known. This 26-block area contains one of the largest and most impressive collections of cast-iron buildings in the United States. The Haughwout Building at 488–492 Broadway is one structure of note. Its cast-iron exterior is designed in the Italianate palazzo style, which some experts believe was based on the Sansovino Library in Venice, Italy. The interior of the building is noteworthy as well: it features a cast-iron skeleton rather than load-bearing masonry walls and was the first building in the city to install a safety elevator for passenger service.

After craning their necks to take in the whimsical details of these historic buildings, visitors can take a short stroll east to Washington Square. Before it was made a public park and parade ground in 1828, the square had gone from being a swampland to a potter's field for yellow-fever victims; in the early 1800's it was used for public hangings. In 1831 a row of 28 Greek Revival town houses, built along the northern perimeter at the end of Fifth Avenue, became the homes of fashionable New Yorkers—among them writer Henry James, who lived for a while in his grandmother's house, the setting for his novel *Washington Square.* In 1889 a wooden memorial designed by Stanford White was erected in the park to commemorate the centennial of George Washington's inauguration as the nation's first president. Three years later it was replaced by the existing stone arch, which dominates the entrance to the park from Fifth Avenue.

When the weather is good, Washington Square becomes a multicultural playground for New Yorkers. While some prefer the mental challenge of a game of chess, others are content to watch a passing parade of people that includes jugglers, mimes, and skateboarders who come here to show off their skills. A short walk north from the square leads to cobblestoned Washington Mews—a lovely lane lined with homes that were once stables. These tiny houses, with their window boxes, remind many visitors of London, England.

Just as Washington Square serves as a landmark for the downtown area, Times Square in midtown Manhattan anchors the Broadway theater district. This has been the heart of American theater for more than a century. Despite periodic cries of despair over diminishing audiences and the occasional disappearance of one beloved stage or another, there are still more than 30 theaters flourishing in the district. Clustered primarily west of Broadway between West 44th and West 53rd streets, some of the most notable theaters are the 1924 Byzantine-styled Martin Beck Theatre, where Eugene O'Neill, Arthur Miller, and Tennessee Williams saw premiere productions of their plays; the Shubert Theatre, where Barbra Streisand made her 1962 debut; and the ornately decorated 1903 Lyceum, the city's oldest surviving theater. Smaller and more avant-garde Off-Broadway theaters are strung out along West 42nd Street's Theater Row. Greenwich Village and the East Village boast their own collections of Off-Off-Broadway theaters—usually presenting smaller productions that feature controversial or offbeat topics.

Beyond midtown lies the Upper East Side's historic district of stately town houses, museums, expensive shops, and landmark buildings. The preeminent shopping thoroughfare is Fifth Avenue. Although the avenue extends from Washington Square all the way uptown to 138th Street, one popular section lies between Rockefeller Center and St. Patrick's Cathedral—one an icon of business and the other a symbol of mankind's yearning for the spiritual. At the end of the 19th century the street was mainly residential, and author Edith

LANDMARK BUILDING
The Empire State Building, below, dwarfs the surrounding structures. Although no longer the tallest building in the world, this Art Deco masterpiece, made of limestone and steel, is truly one of the grandest.

CATCH OF THE DAY
Vendors at the Fulton Fish Market, right, work at a frantic pace to prepare their wares for the predawn crowd that comes to purchase fresh fish. The Brooklyn Bridge is barely visible through the thick fog.

STREET FARE WITH A TWIST
A street vendor in Union Square's Farmer Market, above, hawks pretzels made by hand in Lancaster, Pennsylvania.

WORLD-CLASS ANTICS
The World Trade Center, right, has attracted a number of daredevils, who have walked a tightrope strung between the two towers, parachuted from the top, and scaled the outside of the building.

Wharton described the houses that lined it as being "in an orderly procession like a young ladies' boarding school taking its daily exercise."

Today Fifth Avenue is a bastion of both wealth and power. Rockefeller Center, an early urban development success story, comprises 22 acres of land on which sit 12 landmark buildings. Radio City Music Hall, the largest indoor theater in the United States, is part of the complex. This impressive Art Deco building, put up in 1932 by architect Edward Durrell Stone, was conceived by Samuel Lionel "Roxy" Rothafel, best known for his movie theaters. One aspect of the music hall's design was inspired by a sunrise Rothafel saw while traveling on an ocean liner across the Atlantic. He succeeded in the realization of his vision: the ceiling of the auditorium has been described as resembling the aurora borealis, a sunburst, and rays of sunlight at dawn. To view the interior, visitors can either attend a performance or go on a tour.

A MULTITUDE OF MUSEUMS This is a city of museums, and there seems to be one for every taste. To name but a few, there are the Museum of Bronx History, the Museum of American Illustration, the Museum of Broadcasting, the Museum of Colored Glass and Light, the Museum of Holography, and the Museum of the American Piano.

The Museum of Modern Art at 11 West 53rd Street has one of the world's best collections of modern masterpieces—paintings, sculptures,

26

prints, drawings, films and videos, as well as architectural and industrial designs. The five levels of exhibition space display representative works from most of the major artists of the art movements from 1880 to the present.

The city's most venerable trove of works is at the Metropolitan Museum of Art, the focal point of Fifth Avenue's Museum Mile. The Met, one of the largest art museums in the world, has a collection of more than 2 million artworks displayed in some 2 million square feet of halls, wings, and annexes.

Among the museum's outstanding displays is the Temple of Dendur, where a soaring skylighted space encloses a first-century B.C. Egyptian temple and gate set by a reflecting pool. The temple was commissioned by the Roman emperor Augustus to honor the deaths of a Nubian chieftain's two sons, who drowned in the Nile River in a wartime skirmish. The second-floor Asian art collection features a re-creation of a Ming scholar's courtyard constructed entirely by Chinese workmen. Ming-period furniture graces the court's interior. Although the airy elegance of the American Wing's Charles Englehard Court invites visitors to sit and relax, its wealth of artwork is irresistible. The wing showcases paintings, sculptures, and decorative art objects from the 17th century to the early 20th century. The collection contains paintings by John Singleton Copley and James McNeill Whistler, silver work by Paul Revere, and one of the world's largest displays of American stained glass.

CENTRAL PARK

Central Park, designed in 1858 by renowned landscape architects Frederick Law Olmsted and Calvert Vaux, encompasses some 843 acres of green space set aside for recreation. It is a natural canvas for city life: New Yorkers and visitors alike picnic at the Sheep Meadow and the Great Lawn, stroll miles of pathways, cycle and skate the pavements, and rent rowboats at Loeb Memorial Boathouse. Special events in the park include the outdoor summer concerts put on by the Metropolitan Opera Company, the New York Philharmonic, and the occasional pop-music star.

Young visitors especially enjoy the puppet shows at the Swedish Cottage and the Heckscher Puppet House. At the Children's Zoo, eager youngsters smile with glee at the prospect of petting goats and other tame animals. Elsewhere, the Central Park Zoo's larger collection of animals includes such creatures as polar bears, snow monkeys, and puffins. There is also an ant farm and a beautiful bird sanctuary. An enchanting carousel, which dates to 1908, has 57 intricately carved horses that beckon both children and adults.

If the 51-block stretch of Fifth Avenue that fronts Central Park is home to the rich and famous, so too is the park's western boulevard: Central Park West is lined with such grand residential buildings as the San Remo, whose twin towers suggest Roman temples, and the fabled Dakota, where John Lennon tragically met his death. Across the street from the Dakota, at the park's 72nd Street entrance, is Strawberry Fields, where lush green lawns, carefully tended gardens, and the flower-strewn *Imagine* mosaic—a memorial to Lennon—have become an irresistible lure to tourists.

LADY LIBERTY
The Statue of Liberty, opposite page, greets boats entering the Upper Bay. A gift from the people of France, the statue was designed by sculptor Frédéric Auguste Bartholdi and completed in Paris in 1884. The statue was then dismantled and shipped to New York. On October 28, 1886, the statue was formally dedicated by Pres. Grover Cleveland.

VIVA ITALIA
A café on Mulberry Street in Little Italy, below, is appropriately named Caffè Roma. Both Caffè Roma and Ferrara's are renowned for their Italian pastries. Between 1880 and 1915 immigrants from Sicily and Naples settled in the district.

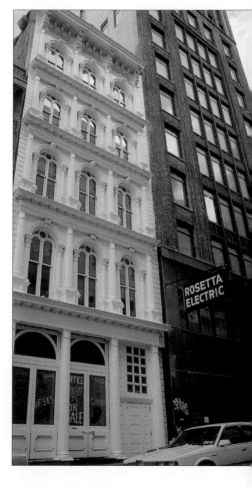

RESTORED SPLENDOR
The 1857 cast-iron facade of a
building in the downtown City
Hall district has been refurbished
to its original beauty.

HISTORIC HARLEM

Harlem, located farther north, has a long history. A Native American village flourished on the fertile banks of the Harlem River long before the Dutch settlers arrived. In 1658 the fledgling Dutch village of Nieuw Haarlem was built by the labors of black slaves brought over from Holland. In the late 19th century Harlem was a fashionable German neighborhood whose streets were lined with elegant brownstone homes and apartment buildings. But as neighborhoods in midtown and downtown became gentrified, African-Americans began to move into Harlem, where the rents were more affordable. By 1920 Harlem was predominantly a black community.

Prior to the Depression, Harlem was one of New York's most vibrant centers of music and nightlife. Alongside casinos and cabarets, such renowned nightclubs as Connie's, the Cotton Club, and Small's Paradise began to attract a steady stream of patrons, both black and white. Today no tour of this neighborhood would be complete without a pilgrimage to the Apollo Theatre. In its heyday the theater boasted the likes of Billie Holiday, Duke Ellington, Count Basie, and Dizzie Gillespie among its performers. Forced to close in 1976 because of declining revenues, the theater has been refurbished and was reopened in 1989.

Harlem's St. Nicholas Historical District contains some of Manhattan's most outstanding examples of Victorian town houses. The prestigious architectural firm McKim, Mead & White designed the neo–Italian Renaissance row on the north side of 139th Street. The street is also the location of Striver's Row, which supposedly got its name because, by 1919, the street was attracting ambitious African-American families who worked hard to improve their lot in life. Some of the famous people who lived in the district include composers Eubie Blake and Noble Sissle, and writer Claude McKay. The Studio Museum in Harlem, now a leading black cultural center, has grown from a small room above a liquor store into a gallery and a distinguished repository of contemporary African-American art and Caribbean folk art.

In the 1930's jazz musicians began using "the Big Apple" to refer to New York, and especially Harlem, as the jazz capital of the world. But some people say the city's nickname was coined a decade earlier by a horse-racing writer for *The Morning Telegraph*, who overheard stable hands refer to New York racecourses as the Big Apple. The writer liked the sound of the moniker and renamed his column "Around the Big Apple." Today the nickname is synonymous with New York—a metropolis that is limitless in scope and ripe for excitement.

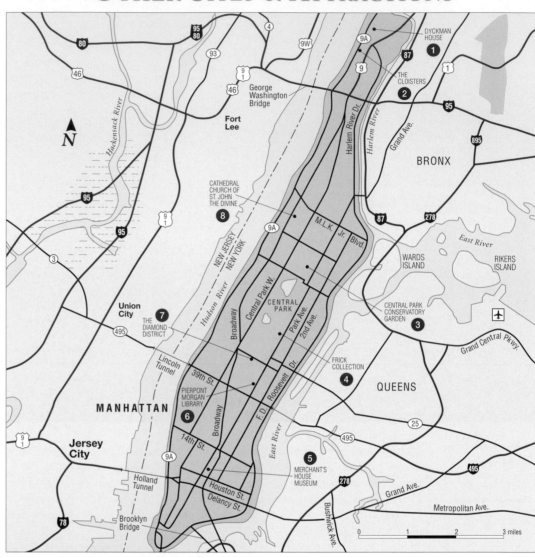

A sculpture depicting Christ in Glory surrounded by the seven lamps and the seven stars of St. John's revelation, below, is the centerpiece of the tympanum, located above the center portal of the Cathedral Church of St. John the Divine.

❶ DYCKMAN HOUSE

This brick-and-wood 1783 Dutch farmhouse, with its herb garden and smokehouse, has been authentically restored and furnished with period pieces. Set on a fieldstone foundation, the house is distinguished by the overhanging eaves and gambrel roof of the Dutch Colonial style. The house once belonged to the Dyckman family, a prominent farming clan who at one time owned more than 450 acres of Upper Manhattan. Located at 4881 Broadway.

❷ THE CLOISTERS

Set on a high rocky bluff overlooking the Hudson River and the New Jersey Palisades, this museum is a harmonious composite of architectural elements from French and Spanish monasteries. It houses the Metropolitan Museum of Art's medieval collection of religious and other artifacts, including the magnificent unicorn tapestries. Located in Fort Tryon Park.

③ CENTRAL PARK CONSERVATORY GARDEN

Visitors enter this part of Central Park through ornate wrought-iron gates that once guarded the sumptuous Cornelius Vanderbilt II mansion and were donated to the city in 1939 by Gertrude Vanderbilt Whitney. The garden originated as a Works Progress Administration project during the Depression, and was restored by the nonprofit Central Park Conservancy in the 1980's. Three formal gardens are graced with fountains, encircled by statues of ladies dancing hand in hand. Located at Fifth Ave. and 105th St.

④ FRICK COLLECTION

A world-class collection of art is housed in one of Fifth Avenue's great mansions, built in 1914 in the neoclassical style for coke-and-steel baron Henry Clay Frick, who was also an avid art collector. The museum, which retains the intimate flavor of a wealthy art patron's home, is graced with European paintings that range primarily from the Renaissance period to the end of the 19th century. The museum also contains an excellent collection of small Renaissance bronzes, enamels, and 18th-century French furniture. Located at 1 E. 70th St.

⑤ MERCHANT'S HOUSE MUSEUM

In the days when the surrounding Bond Street neighborhood was a posh area in which to reside, this 1832 house was built by a hat merchant and

A bedroom, furnished with a 19th-century four-poster bed, above, is one of several rooms in the Dyckman House that are open to the public.

sold to Seabury Tredwell for $18,000. It stayed in the Tredwell family until 1933. Visitors can tour the house, which is furnished with fine pieces in the late Federal, American Empire, and Victorian styles. Located at 29 E. 4th St.

⑥ PIERPONT MORGAN LIBRARY

The austere facade of this 1906 palazzo hides a sumptuous interior where banker J. Pierpont Morgan kept his priceless collection of rare books and documents. Among its possessions, the library has a Gutenberg Bible, autographed manuscripts from the Middle Ages and Renaissance period, and ancient written records dating to the Assyrian and Babylonian civilizations. Located at 29 E. 36th St.

⑦ THE DIAMOND DISTRICT

One of Manhattan's many lively commercial enclaves, this one-block area is the center of the diamond trade, where millions of dollars in gems are traded every day. The traders are primarily Hasidic Jews who work from the district's bazaarlike stores. Each store is crammed with dozens of tiny booths displaying the gleaming gems. Located on W. 47th St. between Fifth and Sixth avenues.

⑧ CATHEDRAL CHURCH OF ST. JOHN THE DIVINE

This French Gothic edifice has been under construction since 1892, and it is estimated that it will cost at least another $400 million and take 50 more years to complete. Among the cathedral's early benefactors were J. P. Morgan and John D. Rockefeller. Its nave is 601 feet long and the church itself covers an area of 21,000 square feet. When it is finished, the building, which is the cathedral of the Episcopalian Diocese of New York, will be the world's largest Gothic cathedral. Located at 1047 Amsterdam Ave.

An elegant doorway leads into the 1832 Merchant's House Museum, left, once known also as the Seabury Tredwell House. Although the family was wealthy in its day, the last surviving member was Gertrude Tredwell, who died in genteel poverty in 1933. The elderly spinster made few, if any, changes to the ancestral home during her lifetime.

GREATER MIAMI

With a nostalgic tip of the hat to its resort image of the past, Miami strides boldly into the future.

It was a spray of orange blossoms, according to one version of Miami's founding, that inspired oil baron Henry Flagler to extend his railroad to a small settlement on the shores of Biscayne Bay. In January 1895 Julia Tuttle, widow of a Cleveland industrialist, sent Flagler some freshly picked flowers, hoping to convince him of southern Florida's development potential. An unusual freeze that winter had devastated the citrus crop upstate near Palm Beach, where Flagler had already opened a fancy resort. However, at the tip of the peninsula, where Tuttle owned a large tract of land, the weather was warm and pleasant. Enthralled, Flagler ordered his railroad construction crews to continue south to the bay. Three months after the first train pulled into the area in April 1896, the city of Miami was incorporated, and what would soon become America's greatest winter resort was born.

A lot has changed since those days when the city was just a few houses clustered around the mouth of the Miami River. The small coastal town

RIDING THE RAILS
Miami's Metromover, above, is composed of individual motorized cars that run on top of a 4.4-mile elevated track that loops around downtown Miami and also goes to the Brickell and Omni business districts. Stops include Bayside Marketplace, Miami Arena, and numerous downtown Miami hotels.

HOLIDAY HAVEN
Overleaf: South Beach's timeless allure is summed up in the sight of a 1950's Packard parked in front of the elegant entrance to an Art Deco hotel. The architectural detail of a tropical scene, right, graces the exterior of The Gallery, one of the newly renovated hotels on Ocean Drive.

has grown into a glittering metropolis. It has become not just a magnet for sunseekers and retirees, but also the world's biggest cruise port and a center of international business.

From the 1920's to the 1960's, Miami was the nation's premier winter resort area. Developers dredged tons of sand from Biscayne Bay and used it to stabilize the strip of mangrove-covered sandbars offshore, thus creating Miami Beach. In 1925 some 481 hotels and apartments were built along the beach, making Miami Beach a mecca for sun worshipers. Some of the most exclusive hotels opened their doors in November and closed in May. Racetracks and prestigious restaurants operated only when winter raged in northern climes. The area's popularity drew new residents as well. The upper-class suburb of Coral Gables, a planned community designed by George Edgar Merrick in the 1920's, is situated on land that was a grapefruit plantation. Many of the lavish homes built in Coral Gables were designed in the Spanish Revival style.

LATIN INFLUENCE

The city of Miami is one of 29 municipalities in the Greater Miami area, and it bears little resemblance to what it looked like 50, or even 25, years ago. What distinguishes it perhaps more than any other feature is its indelible Hispanic flavor. When Fidel Castro swept into power in Havana in 1959, Cuban immigrants began to trickle in. By the 1980's the flow had grown to a veritable torrent, and now more than half the residents of Miami are Hispanic and many of them are Cuban. Miami's Little Havana neighborhood, situated near the city's downtown core, is the traditional center of the Cuban community. Signs along the main street, Calle Ocho (Eighth Street), attest to its proud heritage. Shoppers walk to the *carniceria* to buy meat, and knots of residents gather outside coffee shops to sip tiny cups of café cubano and discuss the issues of the day. Elderly Cubans play dominoes and chess in Maximo Gomez Park. An eternal flame burns in Cuban Memorial Plaza in honor of Cubans who lost their lives at the Bay of Pigs, the 1961 U.S. government-backed invasion of Cuba.

Although English is still the language of business, a stroll along the streets of Miami soon reveals that many of its inhabitants are speaking Spanish. Many of Miami's companies require employees who work with the public to be bilingual. Visitors can sample Cuban/Spanish cuisine at one of the many restaurants that grace the area. The Cuban staple of *picadillo*—ground beef with onion, olives, and spices—served with black beans, rice, and fried plantains, is a popular meal even in non-Cuban households. And the *guayabera,* an embroidered shirt, is often worn by Miami businessmen instead of the traditional suit and tie. This more casual style of dressing suits the climate and looks right at home in this subtropical city.

Miami declined as a tourist hot spot in the early 1980's, but today it is more popular than ever. The city has learned to cope with the social unrest

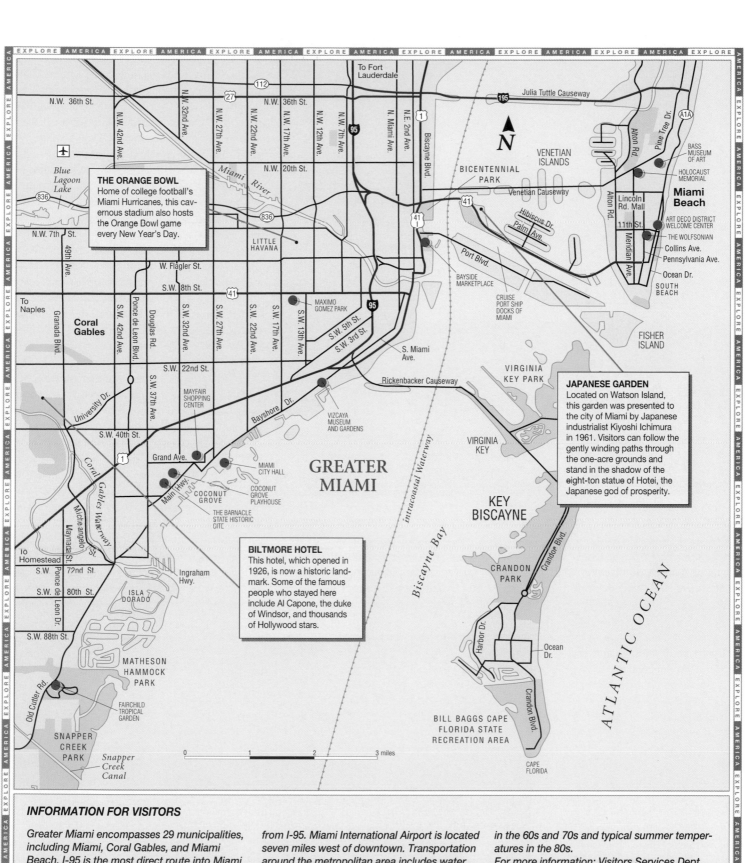

To Fort Lauderdale

112

27

N.W. 36th St.

N.W. 36th St.

N.W. 32nd Ave.

N.W. 42nd Ave.

N.W. 27th Ave.

N.W. 22nd Ave.

N.W. 17th Ave.

N.W. 12th Ave.

N.W. 7th Ave.

N. Miami Ave.

N.E. 2nd Ave.

Biscayne Blvd.

95

1

195

Julia Tuttle Causeway

A1A

N

Pine Tree Dr.

Alton Rd.

BASS MUSEUM OF ART

HOLOCAUST MEMORIAL

Miami Beach

VENETIAN ISLANDS

BICENTENNIAL PARK

Venetian Causeway

Hibiscus Dr.

Palm Ave.

Lincoln Rd. Mall

11th St.

ART DECO DISTRICT WELCOME CENTER

THE WOLFSONIAN

Collins Ave.

Pennsylvania Ave.

Ocean Dr.

SOUTH BEACH

Meridian Ave.

41

N.W. 20th St.

Miami River

836

LITTLE HAVANA

THE ORANGE BOWL
Home of college football's Miami Hurricanes, this cavernous stadium also hosts the Orange Bowl game every New Year's Day.

✈

Blue Lagoon Lake

836

N.W. 7th St.

49th Ave.

W. Flagler St.

S.W. 8th St.

41

S.W. 5th St.

S.W. 3rd St.

MAXIMO GOMEZ PARK

95

S. Miami Ave.

BAYSIDE MARKETPLACE

Port Blvd.

CRUISE PORT SHIP DOCKS OF MIAMI

FISHER ISLAND

To Naples

Coral Gables

Granada Blvd.

Ponce de Leon Blvd.

Douglas Rd.

S.W. 42nd Ave.

S.W. 32nd Ave.

S.W. 27th Ave.

S.W. 22nd Ave.

S.W. 17th Ave.

S.W. 13th Ave.

S.W. 22nd St.

S.W. 37th Ave.

University Dr.

MAYFAIR SHOPPING CENTER

S.W. 40th St.

Grand Ave.

Main Hwy.

COCONUT GROVE

MIAMI CITY HALL

COCONUT GROVE PLAYHOUSE

THE BARNACLE STATE HISTORIC SITE

Bayshore Dr.

VIZCAYA MUSEUM AND GARDENS

Rickenbacker Causeway

GREATER MIAMI

Intracoastal Waterway

VIRGINIA KEY PARK

VIRGINIA KEY

KEY BISCAYNE

JAPANESE GARDEN
Located on Watson Island, this garden was presented to the city of Miami by Japanese industrialist Kiyoshi Ichimura in 1961. Visitors can follow the gently winding paths through the one-acre grounds and stand in the shadow of the eight-ton statue of Hotei, the Japanese god of prosperity.

Biscayne Bay

BILTMORE HOTEL
This hotel, which opened in 1926, is now a historic landmark. Some of the famous people who stayed here include Al Capone, the duke of Windsor, and thousands of Hollywood stars.

Coral Gables Waterway

1

Michelangelo St.

Maynada St.

To Homestead

S.W. 72nd St.

S.W. 80th St.

S.W. Ponce de Leon Dr.

Ingraham Hwy.

ISLA DORADO

CRANDON PARK

Crandon Blvd.

Harbor Dr.

Ocean Dr.

ATLANTIC OCEAN

S.W. 88th St.

MATHESON HAMMOCK PARK

Old Cutler Rd.

FAIRCHILD TROPICAL GARDEN

SNAPPER CREEK PARK

Snapper Creek Canal

BILL BAGGS CAPE FLORIDA STATE RECREATION AREA

Crandon Blvd.

CAPE FLORIDA

0   1   2   3 miles

INFORMATION FOR VISITORS

Greater Miami encompasses 29 municipalities, including Miami, Coral Gables, and Miami Beach. I-95 is the most direct route into Miami from the north. Travelers from the west can take Hwy. 41 across the state. Seven causeways link Miami and Miami Beach; I-195 (Julia Tuttle Causeway) and I-395 (MacArthur Causeway) are easily reached by expressways

from I-95. Miami International Airport is located seven miles west of downtown. Transportation around the metropolitan area includes water taxis, buses, and a 21-mile elevated rail system called the Metrorail, which serves downtown Miami and extends west to Hialeah and south to Kendall. Miami enjoys a subtropical climate year-round with average winter temperatures

in the 60s and 70s and typical summer temperatures in the 80s.
For more information: Visitors Services Dept. of the Greater Miami Convention and Visitors Bureau, 701 Brickell Ave., Suite 2700, Miami, FL 33131; 305-539-3063 or 800-933-8448.

EXPLORE AMERICA EXPLORE AMERICA EXPLORE AMERICA EXPLORE AMERICA EXPLORE AMERICA EXPLORE AMERICA EXPLORE AMERICA EXPLORE AMERICA EXPLORE

GREATER MIAMI 35

two decades ago, has been transformed into glamorous South Beach. In downtown Miami, the 32-acre Bayfront Park has been redesigned by Isamu Noguchi, one of the country's foremost sculptors. The First Union Financial Center on Biscayne Avenue is not far from where Flagler constructed the Royal Palm Hotel, Miami's first major resort. The 751-foot-high building—the tallest office tower in Florida—presides over a downtown crammed with skyscrapers. The downtown area is familiar to many Americans as the backdrop for numerous television series and films. Miami has a foreign trade of about $34 billion, and in the early 1990's was ranked 10th on *Fortune* magazine's list of best cities for business. Its airport receives and dispatches more international passengers than any other airport in the nation with the exception of Kennedy Airport in New York.

PARADISE ON EARTH

What makes today's Miami such a popular vacation destination is its remarkably diverse attractions. Its pristine natural beauty, vibrant neighborhoods, professional sports teams, and modern centers of culture and art draw millions of tourists to the city every year. When the temperature hovers at 65°F in mid-February and moonlight plays on the gentle waves of Biscayne Bay, it is easy to believe that Miami is considered a paradise on earth.

Visitors gravitate to South Beach's famous Art Deco district, which in the 1920's and '30's was a middle-class tourist resort. The whimsical designs of the hotels, which have a streamlined look and stylized, geometric ornamentation, were influenced

MEDITERRANEAN MASTERPIECE
John Deering's grand Italian Renaissance villa, Vizcaya, above, cost an estimated $20 million to build in 1916. Saddled with heavy taxes, Deering's family sold off most of the land. In 1952 the house and the remaining 28 acres were bought by Dade County for $1 million and opened to the public. Every year some 20,000 people attend the Italian Renaissance Festival, famous for its chess game in which people stand in for the chess pieces.

that often accompanies rapid urban growth into a large multicultural city. During the past 20 years, revitalization programs have had an enormous impact on Greater Miami. Examples abound. The southern tip of Miami Beach, dotted with low-rent hotels and decrepit apartment buildings a mere

BOATBUILDER'S HOME
The Barnacle, right, built by Comdr. Ralph Munroe, overlooks Biscayne Bay. The 1891 house, located on the five-acre Barnacle State Historic Site, is furnished with period pieces. The commodore had a passion for building yachts and a replica of one of his boats, the 28-foot Egret, *is moored in the bay.*

by works of art that were displayed at the *Exposition des Art Décoratifs et Industriels Modernes*, which was held in Paris, France, in 1925. The Art Deco buildings' sleek modernistic exteriors drew vacationers seeking escape from the gloom and doom of the Depression years. Recent conservation efforts have helped in getting many of these splendid buildings restored to their original condition and painted in pastels. Porthole windows, wraparound corners, vertical fins, and horizontal banding make this famed strip of South Beach an architectural fantasyland and a much-favored backdrop for many commercial photographers on assignment for fashion magazines. A popular pastime of

South Beach visitors is to sit under an umbrella in one of the sidewalk cafés on Ocean Drive and watch the passing parade of fashion types.

Ocean Drive, the signature street of South Beach, is one long stretch of dreamy Art Deco buildings that open onto a succession of sidewalk cafés. Tanned inline skaters, camera-carrying Midwesterners, and a host of travelers from Europe and South America give the district an international flavor. At night revelers stream into the cafés and clubs and spill over to neighboring streets. Washington Avenue is the late-night heart of the district, with some of its bars and nightclubs not opening until midnight and only shutting down at 4:00 or 5:00 a.m.

NEVER FORGOTTEN
Artist Kenneth Treister's Holocaust Memorial, left, in Miami Beach was created in memory of the 6 million Jewish victims of the Holocaust. The memorial is composed of a 42-foot-tall bronze sculpture surrounded by a black granite wall, which is hung with archival photographs and engraved with the names of people who were killed in the Nazi concentration camps.

HOLIDAY FOR BODY AND SOUL
The white, sandy beaches of Miami Beach, below, are only one of its attractions. The city is home to the Bass Museum of Art, which houses a permanent collection of old masters, and the Wolfsonian, a museum that focuses on decorative and propaganda arts.

a Miami suburb along the bay. Miami City Hall is located here in a building that was originally the seaplane terminal for Pan American World Airways. It later became a restaurant before it was turned into the city's municipal headquarters. Such new developments as CocoWalk and, more recently, Streets of Mayfair, are complexes of chic upscale shops, restaurants, bars, and cinemas, built around an open courtyard. The area has excellent local repertory theater in the Coconut Grove Playhouse, and sailboats and motor yachts cruise along the neighborhood's marina-lined shore year-round.

DREAM PALACE

Perhaps the most famous site in Coconut Grove is Vizcaya Museum and Gardens, a beautiful Italian Renaissance palace that overlooks Biscayne Bay. The mansion was constructed between 1914 and 1916 to be the winter home of International Harvester heir James Deering. Told by doctors to move to Florida for

THRILL OF THE GAME
Maximo Gomez Park, above, provides the perfect spot for a friendly game of dominoes.

Rivaling Ocean Drive as a center of activity in South Beach is Lincoln Road and its bustling pedestrian mall. Known as the Fifth Avenue of the South when it was constructed in the 1920's, the street has recently undergone a stunning multimillion-dollar face-lift. It has become the cultural heart of South Florida, with exclusive art galleries and antique shops, two concert halls, the Miami City Ballet, and several television and recording company offices and studios. The mall is also home to some excellent eateries. In some of them, diners can enjoy a meal under the stars in the mall's palm-dotted median.

No section of Greater Miami revels in its modernity as much as downtown Miami. Its star attraction is also one of its most recent developments: the Bayside Marketplace, situated on Biscayne Bay at the foot of the bridge leading to the port of Miami. This complex encompasses more than 150 shops, restaurants, and clubs, as well as a busy marina that opens onto a waterfront plaza where bands perform at night. During the day, sightseeing trips take visitors out by boat onto the Atlantic Ocean.

South of downtown lies the neighborhood of Coconut Grove,

FLORA OF FLORIDA
Visitors who stroll through the conservatory at the Fairchild Tropical Garden, right, can expect to see everything from exotic flowering trees and sunken gardens to still pools and quiet grassy spaces. A tram takes visitors for longer jaunts through the grounds of the botanical garden.

his health, the lifelong bachelor traveled to Europe accompanied by decorator-designer Paul Chalfin in order to purchase the finest furniture and ornaments for his new 70-room home. When they returned they brought with them an eclectic mix of period pieces—tapestries, beds, tables, and chairs—ranging in style from Renaissance and neoclassic to Baroque and rococo.

The villa is located at the end of a long drive through a subtropical hummock. Its loggias and central courtyard take advantage of the bay's cooling breezes. An unusual feature of the 10-acre estate is a boat-shaped island called Stone Barge, which serves as a breakwater. Made from rocks discarded from the site when the villa was being constructed, Stone Barge is decorated with sculptures by Stirling Calder, whose son Alexander Calder became a world-renowned artist and sculptor.

About a 15-minute drive south of Vizcaya lies the 83-acre Fairchild Tropical Garden, site of a world-class botanical garden named for plant explorer David Fairchild. On display here are more than 500 varieties of palm trees from as far away as Brazil, Borneo, and the Seychelles Islands, as well as cycads, leafy vines, and flowering trees. A 16,000-square-foot conservatory houses a community of fragile tropical plants, including the red-trunked ceiling wax palm and the unusual bat plant, which coincidentally blossoms around Halloween with reddish brown blooms in the shape of bats.

YOUTHFUL VIGOR

As the orange sun begins its slow descent into the ocean, the lights of Miami's skyscrapers and the luxurious cruise ships docked in port illuminate the city and the shoreline. Greater Miami is a relative youngster among the urban areas rooted along the Eastern Seaboard: the city of Miami itself just celebrated its centennial in 1996. Once a retreat for the well-heeled, the vibrant metropolis, infused with new residents from all parts of the globe, offers visitors a chance to soak up the Florida sun and savor the city's multifaceted attractions.

BEACH ARCHITECTURE
Some of the lifeguard stands along the stretches of Miami Beach, above, are painted in eye-catching colors. There are more than 15 miles of tropical public beaches in Greater Miami.

OTHER SITES & ATTRACTIONS

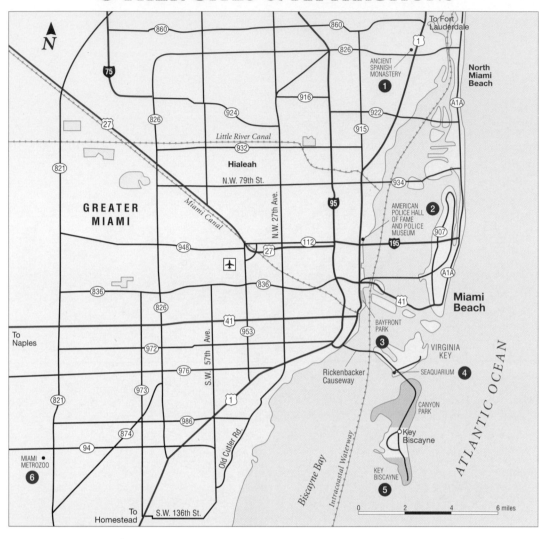

The islands of Biscayne Bay, below, including Key Biscayne, provide a welcome respite from the hubbub of downtown Miami.

❶ ANCIENT SPANISH MONASTERY

The Ancient Spanish Monastery Cloisters of the Church of St. Bernard de Clairvaux, the oldest building in the Western Hemisphere still standing, was transported from Segovia, Spain, to Miami in 1925. Constructed in 1141, the monastery was occupied by Cistercian monks until the mid-1800's. It was used as a stable until it was purchased by newspaper publisher William Randolph Hearst, who had it dismantled stone by stone and shipped to a Brooklyn warehouse in 10,751 straw-lined crates. The crates languished in a warehouse until the 1950's, when the city of Miami purchased them from Hearst's estate. Reassembled in 1954, the structure is considered a prime example of Romanesque and Cistercian architecture and has a delicate limestone cloister with 52 arches. Its chapter house is composed of 75 interlocking stone arches. Five seven-ton double arches support the roof of the rectory. The monastery is used as an Episcopal church, but visitors are welcome to tour the building when services are not being held. Paintings, sculptures, and furniture are on display inside the church. Located at 16711 W. Dixie Hwy. in North Miami Beach.

2 AMERICAN POLICE HALL OF FAME AND POLICE MUSEUM

Crime and punishment are the focus of this museum. Police equipment on display includes billy clubs, tear gas guns, leg irons, and bulletproof vests, including one that still has four bullets embedded in it. A number of police vehicles are exhibited, among them an antique police car from 1937, a SWAT team assault vehicle, and the futuristic police pursuit car that was used in the science-fiction film *Blade Runner*. A 400-ton marble memorial is engraved with the names of more than 6,000 policemen who have lost their lives in the line of duty since 1960. Execution devices on display include an electric chair, gas chamber, noose, and guillotine. Located at 3801 Biscayne Blvd. in Miami.

3 BAYFRONT PARK

In the early 1980's Isamu Noguchi, a prominent American sculptor, was commissioned by the city of Miami to redesign and refurbish this 32-acre waterfront park, which has become a popular place for walks. The AT&T Amphitheater and the Tina Hills Pavilion are venues for musical and theatrical events. The park also contains several notable monuments and sculptures, including the Laser Light Tower, the largest freestanding laser light in the world. A statue of Christopher Columbus was a gift from the Italian government, and the astronauts of the space shuttle *Challenger* are remembered with a memorial. Located along North Biscayne Blvd. in Miami.

4 SEAQUARIUM

The Seaquarium's 100 species of marine life entertain more than 700,000 visitors a year. This 38-acre park is divided into four show sections. One of the stars of the Killer Whale Show is Lolita, a whale that weighs more than 7,000 pounds. Porpoises cavort in the lagoon where the television show *Flipper* was filmed in the 1960's and 1970's. Reef aquariums dis-

play many species of colorful fish that are found in the waters of the Atlantic and Caribbean. Located on Biscayne Bay off the Rickenbacker Causeway.

5 KEY BISCAYNE

With its miles of sandy oceanfront, a marina, golf course, tennis center, two large public parks, and a historic lighthouse, Key Biscayne is a popular recreation site. Visitors to Oceanfront Crandon Park enjoy its sandy beach and picnic areas. The 18-hole Crandon Park Golf Course is one of the most difficult courses in Miami. Bill Baggs Cape Florida State Recreation Area occupies the southern end of the island. At its tip stands a brick lighthouse that was attacked in 1836 during the Seminole Wars; marauding Indians set fire to the structure, killing the lightkeeper. One of Miami's most historic structures, the lighthouse, along with a replica of the original lightkeeper's house, can be visited. Located east of Miami off the Rickenbacker Causeway.

6 MIAMI METROZOO

One of the country's most renowned zoos, this cageless facility is home to a pair of Komodo dragons, the world's largest living lizards. Nearly 10 feet in length, the dragons are found in the wild only on a few islands in Indonesia. Another popular attraction at the zoo is the replica of an Angkor Wat temple in Cambodia—complete with intricate outer carvings and statues—where Bengal tigers roam free. The zoo's lowland gorillas are popular with visitors, as are its African warthogs, the type featured in the movie *The Lion King*. Disney animators based many of their original drawings on these animals. Other animals in the zoo include koala bears, Siamese crocodiles, bongo antelopes, African elephants, and one Asian bull elephant. A two-mile-long trail winds through a section of the zoo's 740 acres, and an elevated monorail provides visitors with an aerial view of the African plains and other animal habitats. Located at 12400 S.W. 152 St. in Miami.

The Bayside Marketplace, above, a 16-acre district of restaurants, sidewalk cafés, and stores, is part of Bayfront Park.

An orangutan, left, is one of the many animals that roam free at the Miami Metrozoo. More than 275 animal species inhabit the zoo. Although badly damaged by Hurricane Andrew in August 1992, the zoo recovered quickly; only its state-of-the-art aviary has yet to be rebuilt.

ATLANTA

Beneath this city's hustle and bustle lies a fascinating mix of Southern grace and urban sophistication.

Until the rise of the railroads, few settlers ventured forth on Georgia's Piedmont Plateau where it lies at the foot of the Appalachian Mountains. Except for a couple of forts built to suppress the Creek Nation during the War of 1812 and a cabin erected by a homesteader near the Chattahoochee River in 1833, this wild land was left to the Indians. When newcomers arrived in Georgia, they tended to cluster in the coastal ports and along navigable inland waterways, or set down roots in the fertile farmland. The backwoods, with their piney thickets, granite ridges, and rivers that sliced through deep valleys, discouraged permanent settlement.

In 1837, when the Georgia legislature voted to extend the Western & Atlantic Railroad lines south from Tennessee to the site of a Cherokee village in Georgia called Standing Peachtree, there was little enthusiasm for the town that would take root there. Even its name suggested limited room for growth: Terminus, the end of the line. Said one shortsighted W&A engineer: "The terminus will be a good location for one tavern, a blacksmith shop, a grocery store and nothing else."

A GAZEBO OF ONE'S OWN
Overleaf: The colonnaded gazebo in Piedmont Park, next to a cool lake and a weeping willow tree, is a perfect place for an Atlantan to sit and read for awhile. The Atlanta Botanical Garden is located at the northern tip of the park.

SOFT DRINK CLASSIC
A collection of familiar items, below, advertises the soft drink that will forever be associated with Atlanta. The original recipe for Coca-Cola, developed in 1886, was based on cocaine from the coca leaf and caffeine-rich extracts of the kola nut. The cocaine was removed from the formula in 1905. The World of Coca-Cola Atlanta, located at 55 Martin Luther King Jr. Drive, displays soft drink memorabilia from the early days.

Few American cities have gone so far with so little in their favor. Against long odds and all logic, Terminus evolved into Atlanta—with a population of 425,200 and another 3 million in metro Atlanta. It is known as the cultural and economic axis of the American South; headquarters of Ted Turner's global communications empire, built around the Cable News Network; the site of the 1996 Olympic Games; and the birthplace of Martin Luther King Jr. Famous Atlantans include W.E.B. Du Bois, the celebrated African-American editor and author who founded the National Association for the Advancement of Colored People (NAACP); and John Pemberton, the pharmacist whose syrupy coca leaf and kola nut headache remedy became the basis for Coca-Cola's formula. The city boasts four professional sports teams, 29 institutions of higher learning, a symphony orchestra, and buildings that house branch offices of 90 percent of the Fortune 500 companies.

Atlanta's starkly modern skyline is anchored by the glistening Peachtree Center, a 14-block complex made up of three towering hotels, plus office buildings, restaurants, retail stores, and a 6-million-square-foot market center, all connected by covered or enclosed walkways. The city's venerable 185-acre Piedmont Park—site of a world-class botanical garden and such events as the Peachtree Road Race—now has a rival in Atlanta's newest urban playground, the Centennial Olympic Park. This 23-acre park, which is the first center-city park to be built in the country in the last 20 years, has helped revitalize the downtown core. Its forest of vertical water jets provides a stunning setting for the city's annual Arts Festival and free concerts staged by the Atlanta Symphony Orchestra.

EQUESTRIAN OFFICERS
Mounted police, above, are a familiar sight on Atlanta's streets and in its many city parks.

INFORMATION FOR VISITORS

The principal north to south interstates providing access to Atlanta are I-75 and I-85, which merge into a single expressway in the city. I-75/85 intersects with the major east–west route, I-20, in downtown Atlanta. I-285 encircles the city. Hartsfield International Airport is located 10 miles south of downtown, near the intersections of I-75, I-85, and I-285. Amtrak and Greyhound-Trailways provide daily service to Atlanta from all major northern cities. Travel within the city by bus and the light-rail system (MARTA) is easy and convenient. The Atlanta Convention and Visitors Bureau has visitor centers at Underground Atlanta, Peachtree Center Mall, Lenox Square shopping center, and Hartsfield International Airport.
For more information: Atlanta Convention and Visitors Bureau, Suite 100, 233 Peachtree St. NW, Atlanta, GA 30303; 404-521-6600.

44

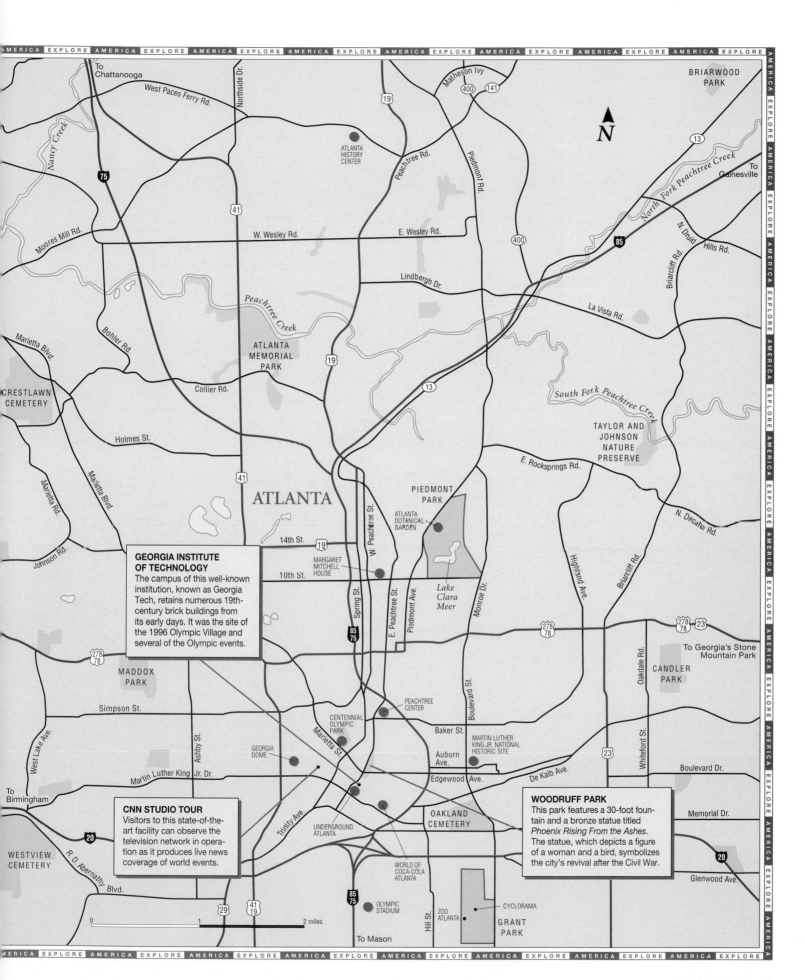

To Chattanooga

West Paces Ferry Rd.

Northside Dr.

Matheson Ivy

BRIARWOOD PARK

N

13

75

41

Nancy Creek

ATLANTA HISTORY CENTER

Peachtree Rd.

Piedmont Rd.

North Fork Peachtree Creek

To Gainesville

85

Moores Mill Rd.

W. Wesley Rd.

E. Wesley Rd.

400

N. Druid Hills Rd.

Bohler Rd.

Lindbergh Dr.

La Vista Rd.

Briarcliff Rd.

Peachtree Creek

ATLANTA MEMORIAL PARK

19

13

South Fork Peachtree Creek

CRESTLAWN CEMETERY

Collier Rd.

TAYLOR AND JOHNSON NATURE PRESERVE

Holmes St.

Marietta Blvd.

E. Rocksprings Rd.

N. Decatur Rd.

Marietta Rd.

41

ATLANTA

PIEDMONT PARK

Highland Ave.

Briarcliff Rd.

Johnson Rd.

14th St.

19

W. Peachtree St.

ATLANTA BOTANICAL GARDEN

278 78

23

GEORGIA INSTITUTE OF TECHNOLOGY
The campus of this well-known institution, known as Georgia Tech, retains numerous 19th-century brick buildings from its early days. It was the site of the 1996 Olympic Village and several of the Olympic events.

10th St.

MARGARET MITCHELL HOUSE

Spring St.

E. Peachtree St.

Piedmont Ave.

Lake Clara Meer

Monroe Dr.

278 78

Oakdale Rd.

CANDLER PARK

To Georgia's Stone Mountain Park

278 78

MADDOX PARK

Simpson St.

Ashby St.

Marietta St.

CENTENNIAL OLYMPIC PARK

PEACHTREE CENTER

Baker St.

Boulevard St.

MARTIN LUTHER KING JR. NATIONAL HISTORIC SITE

23

Whiteford St.

West Lake Ave.

GEORGIA DOME

Martin Luther King Jr. Dr.

Auburn Ave.

De Kalb Ave.

Boulevard Dr.

85 75

CNN STUDIO TOUR
Visitors to this state-of-the-art facility can observe the television network in operation as it produces live news coverage of world events.

Trinity Ave.

Edgewood Ave.

OAKLAND CEMETERY

WOODRUFF PARK
This park features a 30-foot fountain and a bronze statue titled *Phoenix Rising From the Ashes*. The statue, which depicts a figure of a woman and a bird, symbolizes the city's revival after the Civil War.

Memorial Dr.

20

To Birmingham

R.D. Abernathy Blvd.

20

WESTVIEW CEMETERY

UNDERGROUND ATLANTA

WORLD OF COCA-COLA ATLANTA

Glenwood Ave.

0   1   2 miles

29

41 19

85 75

OLYMPIC STADIUM

Hill St.

ZOO ATLANTA

CYCLORAMA

GRANT PARK

To Mason

AMERICA EXPLORE AMERICA EXPLORE AMERICA EXPLORE AMERICA EXPLORE AMERICA EXPLORE AMERICA EXPLORE AMERICA EXPLORE AMERICA EXPLORE AMERICA EXPLORE AMERICA EXPLORE AMERICA EXPLORE AMERICA EXPLORE

ATLANTA 45

THE AUTHOR'S TARA

Atlantan Margaret Mitchell, author of the Pulitzer Prize–winning Gone With the Wind (1936), wrote most of the novel in the house at right. The corner apartment that she shared with her husband from 1925–32 was affectionately referred to as "the dump" by the author. It has been restored and is now open to the public as the Margaret Mitchell House. Mitchell had a low opinion of the novel that made her famous, saying, "It stinks. I don't know why I bother with it, but I've got to have something to do with my time."

STONE MOUNTAIN

The largest bas-relief sculpture in the world (90 by 190 feet), below, depicts Robert E. Lee, Stonewall Jackson, and Jefferson Davis.

Despite its forward-looking ambitions, Atlanta retains the magnolia-and-jasmine-scented ambience of the Old South. The dogwoods, maples, oaks, and sycamores of the verdant plateau act as an emerald understory flecked with crepe myrtle and redbuds, lending an air of seclusion to many of the city's neighborhoods.

The thoroughfares and light-rail transit corridors of modern Atlanta follow to a large extent the winding courses of Indian trails that were tramped out centuries before white settlers arrived. Peachtree Street, the meandering commercial conduit of Atlanta, is one of these. At least 31 other streets use the word Peachtree in their names—the legacy of the village that once occupied this spot.

Underground Atlanta, a six-city-block entertainment zone in the downtown core, is a lively strip of restaurants, nightclubs, and vendors' stalls that owes its existence to an earlier era. In the first part of the century, converging and crisscrossing rail lines created so much congestion—and peril to pedestrians—that in 1929 the city fathers installed a system of bridges and viaducts to raise the streets, creating, for a time, a two-level city. As businesses moved up to the new street level, the

lower tier was abandoned and gradually decayed. In the late 1960's the lower buildings were restored and named Underground Atlanta. Except for a period of economic downturn in the 1980's, the nightlife has flourished there ever since.

BATTLE OF ATLANTA

During the Civil War, few Southern cities suffered as terribly as Atlanta did, but the city wears its scars proudly. A graphic reminder of this grim period in Atlanta's history can be seen in the Atlanta Cyclorama in Grant Park, where the world's largest oil painting depicts the Battle of Atlanta. The battle began at mid-afternoon on July 22, 1864, when Confederate soldiers fought to protect Atlanta from Union forces and struggled vainly to hold on to the factories and railroads that were vital to the Southern cause. The 9,334-pound oil painting, called *Battle of Atlanta,* is the work of 11 European artists, who painted it between 1884 and 1886. It is taller than a four-story building and has a sweeping circumference of 358 feet. A revolving platform provides visitors with a 360-degree view of the massive painting, complete with lighting, sound effects, and narration in five languages.

By the time the city fell to Union forces that fateful summer of 1864, the outcome of the Civil War was a foregone conclusion. Union victories in 1863 at Vicksburg, Mississippi, and Gettysburg, Pennsylvania, had sent the death rattle of the secessionist South reverberating across the land like cannon fire.

It was Gen. William Tecumseh Sherman who uttered the immortal words "War is hell" as he watched the incineration of Jackson, Mississippi. The year before, he had amassed 100,000 troops in Tennessee and crossed into Georgia in what became known as the March to the Sea.

After a month of siege and heavy artillery bombardment, Union troops entered Atlanta, only to find it nearly in ruins. Sherman's onslaught had inflicted heavy damage on the city, but the greatest destruction was wreaked on its factories, trains, and rail lines by retreating Rebel soldiers who were bent on keeping potential military assets out of enemy hands.

Lest the South rise again on the banks of the Chattahoochee River, Sherman ordered the evacuation of the remaining 1,644 citizens, then had his troops set Atlanta afire before they departed for Savannah. Only about 400 of Atlanta's 4,500 buildings survived the flames.

For all its savagery and senselessness, the destruction of Atlanta would prove to be a defining

PEACHTREE TREASURE
The High Museum of Art, above, designed by architect Richard Meier and opened in 1983, was described by the New York Times *as "among the best any city has built in at least a generation." Located at 1280 Peachtree Street N.E., the museum's four stories of galleries contain artworks ranging from 18th-century Oriental ceramics to American oil paintings by artists John Singer Sargent, Albert Bierstadt, and Childe Hassam.*

SYMBOLIC PARK
The 23-acre Centennial Olympic Park, left, was constructed for the 1996 Olympic Games. The urban park was paved with bricks paid for by citizens from around the world, whose names were individually inscribed on the bricks.

SWEET AUBURN

*Auburn Avenue, right, runs
through Atlanta's Sweet Auburn
district. Civil rights leader Martin
Luther King Jr. was born on
January 15, 1929, at 501 Auburn
Avenue. The Martin Luther King Jr.
National Historic Site encompasses
the house, the Ebenezer Baptist
Church, where both King and his
father preached, and King's grave
site. The Nobel Prize–winning minister was assassinated in Memphis,
Tennessee, at the age of 39.*

moment in determining the city's future—one that shaped the sensibilities and character of its inhabitants. Whereas other Southern cities had suffered similar fates during the war and thereafter declined, valiant Atlanta rose from the ashes with a singular force and purpose.

After the 1936 publication of Margaret Mitchell's Civil War masterpiece *Gone With the Wind,* some Atlantans would claim that the stubborn and resilient heroine, Scarlett O'Hara, personified the city. Wrote Mitchell, "Throughout the South for fifty years there would be bitter-eyed women who looked backward, to dead times, to dead men, evoking memories that hurt and were futile, bearing poverty with bitter pride because they had those memories. But Scarlett was never to look back." Like the mistress of Tara, Atlantans looked foward and rebuilt a city that has become the epitome of a vibrant Southern metropolis.

IMPRESSIVE REBIRTH When Sherman returned to the city 14 years after the war, it bore little resemblance to the one his army had besieged. Nearly everything was new: its churches, schools, theaters, and railroads had been rebuilt, and opera houses, hotels, saloons, brothels, and gambling parlors were doing a flourishing business. The citizens threw a lavish ball for Sherman. Even more

surprising: several years later *Atlanta Constitution* editor Henry Grady saluted the general's role in Atlanta's development when he wrote, "I want to say to General Sherman, who is an able man, though some people think he is kind of careless about fire, that from the ashes he left us in 1864 we have raised a brave and beautiful city; that we have caught the sunshine in our homes and built therein not one ignoble prejudice or memory."

While Atlantans may have forgiven Sherman, they did not forget their own leaders. A 15-mile drive east from the Cyclorama leads to the 3,200-acre Stone Mountain Park, where the main attraction is the towering horseback images of three Confederate icons—Robert E. Lee, Stonewall Jackson, and Jefferson Davis—all three of them etched into the three-acre side of the world's largest granite outcropping. A tram carries visitors past the sculpture to the 825-foot summit.

More Civil War accounts and memorabilia are on display in the Atlanta History Center, where exhibits trace the city's history from the time of the Cherokee and Creek Indians up to the present. Visitors can wander through the center's 32 acres of gardens and nature trails, and visit two historic houses: the grand 1928 Swan House, and an 1840's plantation farmhouse and outbuildings, called the Tullie Smith Farm, which provide a glimpse of rural life before the Civil War.

The King Center is located on a 42-acre National Historical Site, which includes the Ebenezer Baptist Church where Martin Luther King Jr. joined his father as co-pastor from 1960–68. Although King was born in Atlanta, he led civil rights battles in Montgomery, Birmingham, Selma, and other Southern bastions of segregation that violently resisted change. It is a point of pride in Atlanta that the violence that tore through many American cities in the 1960's never broke out here.

In 1959 Mayor William Hartsfield declared: "Atlanta is a city too busy to hate." Two years later Atlanta proved him right when its public schools were integrated without any race-related incidents. President Kennedy praised the city's leaders for their "courage, tolerance and, above all, respect for the law." In 1974 Maynard Jackson became the first black mayor of a major Southern city.

Atlanta's resilience and ability to adapt set it apart. It is fitting that the city's seal shows a phoenix rising from its own ashes accompanied by the Latin word *Resurgens,* meaning "rise again." The railroad engineer who predicted that the town of Terminus would never amount to much would be amazed to see the place now.

COMPELLING MEMORIAL

On Auburn Avenue, conflict of another kind is commemorated at the Martin Luther King Jr. Center for Nonviolent Social Change—perhaps Atlanta's most compelling attraction. Each year hundreds of thousands of pilgrims visit the site where the body of the civil rights leader lies entombed in marble above a quiet plaza graced with a reflective pool and an eternal flame.

PEACHTREE EVERYWHERE
The street, above, that runs for miles through the city got its name from the original Creek encampment, which was established on the banks of the Chattahoochee River. The names of 32 avenues, boulevards, roads, and streets share the word Peachtree, creating confusion for many visitors to the city.

NEVER SAY DIE
The mural, left, painted by local artist Del Nichols and on display at the Road to Tara Museum depicts Clark Gable and Vivien Leigh, the stars of the MGM movie Gone With the Wind, *as well as the ghosted portraits of secondary characters from the film. The museum houses* Gone With the Wind *memorabilia, including movie posters, first editions of the novel, and more than 50 dolls dressed to look like characters from the story.* Gone With the Wind *won nine major Oscars and two special Oscars at the 1940 Academy Awards.*

The Wren's Nest House Museum, above, once the home of writer Joel Chandler Harris of Br'er Rabbit fame, was declared a National Historic Landmark in 1976.

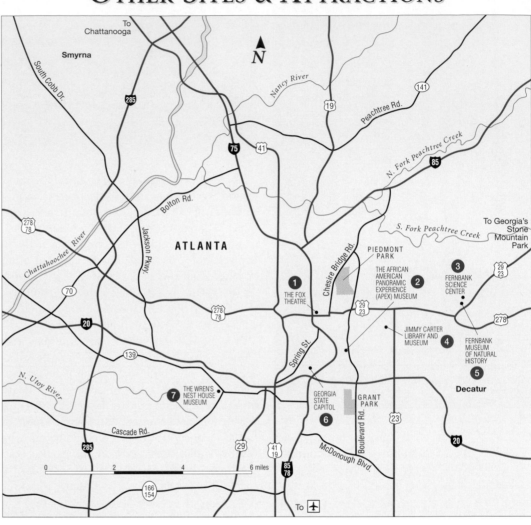

① THE FOX THEATRE

When this ornate theater opened in 1929, it was intended to be a headquarters for the Shriners, but hard times led to a change in plans. The theater's facade, which has, according to one local newspaper, "an almost disturbing grandeur," contains elements of Moorish and Art Deco architectural styles. New York Metropolitan Opera singers once performed regularly at the theater and it is still a frequent stop for touring concerts and Broadway shows. The building is listed on the National Register of Historic Places. Located at 660 Peachtree St. NE.

② THE AFRICAN AMERICAN PANORAMIC EXPERIENCE (APEX) MUSEUM

This 7,500-square-foot building is in the heart of the Martin Luther King Jr. National Historic District, the area of Atlanta where King was born. The museum offers artifacts and a video presentation narrated by Cicely Tyson that relates the history of Auburn Avenue, once the center of black commerce and culture in Atlanta. One exhibit re-creates the interior of the Yates & Milton Drugstore, one of the first African-American-owned businesses in Atlanta.

From their seats aboard an antique trolley car, visitors can watch a multimedia presentation devoted to the history of African-Americans. Located at 135 Auburn Ave. NE.

③ FERNBANK SCIENCE CENTER

Visitors to the Fernbank Science Center can see star shows in the planetarium, look through a telescope in the observatory, and walk through a patch of old-growth forest, which is located behind the science center. A video presentation explains such geological phenomena as volcanoes and earthquakes, and there is an small exhibit of gems and fossils. The planetarium is one of the most technologically sophisticated in the nation, offering numerous shows relating to the solar system. The huge dome of the Fernbank Observatory houses the largest single-optics telescope in the American Southeast. The observatory is open to the public on Thursday and Friday nights, when an astronomer is on hand to answer questions. Paved walking trails wind through the Fernbank Forest and lead to a small pond. Located at 156 Heaton Park Dr. NE.

Lush gardens grace the Jimmy Carter Library and Museum, left, which provides visitors with an impressive view of Atlanta from its site on a hill.

④ JIMMY CARTER LIBRARY AND MUSEUM

The Jimmy Carter Library and Museum sits on Copenhill, where Gen. William Tecumseh Sherman observed and directed his troops during the 1864 Battle of Atlanta. The museum contains a replica of the White House Oval Office as it was when Carter was president, as well as more than 27 million pages of documents and 1.5 million photographs relating to his presidency. Interactive displays allow visitors to ask the former president questions about his political career. Located at 1 Copenhill Ave.

⑤ FERNBANK MUSEUM OF NATURAL HISTORY

The largest museum of natural history in the Southeast explores the origins of the universe and the development of life on earth. Permanent exhibits include the "World of Shells," housed in a 1,000-gallon aquarium. An exhibit on light and sound titled "Spectrum of the Senses" contains hands-on displays. Located at 767 Clifton Rd. NE.

⑥ GEORGIA STATE CAPITOL

Built of Georgia marble and Indiana limestone, this 1889 building has a dome covered with native gold leaf and topped by a 15-foot statue of a female figure holding a torch—a monument to the state's war dead. On the grounds stand statues of well-known Georgian politicians and a sculpture commemorating the 33 black state legislators, who were elected to the House and expelled in 1868 because of their color. The building houses displays relating to the natural sciences, a Hall of Flags, and a Hall of Fame honoring outstanding Georgians. Located on Capitol Hill at Washington St.

⑦ THE WREN'S NEST HOUSE MUSEUM

Joel Chandler Harris wrote some of his famous stories about Uncle Remus and Br'er Rabbit while living in the Wren's Nest, a house the author named after a family of wrens that had built their nest in his mailbox. A youngster during the years leading up to the Civil War, Harris grew fascinated with the tales told by the slaves who lived near his rural Georgia home. After the war he worked as an editor for the *Atlanta Constitution,* and began to write down the stories. In 1879 they were published and the wise old black man Uncle Remus, with his stories about Br'er Rabbit and Br'er Fox, became a literary icon. The Wren's Nest, a National Historic Landmark, is an excellent example of early Queen Anne architecture in the Atlanta region. The two-story structure has a large wraparound porch decorated with gingerbread woodwork. Located at 1050 Ralph D. Abernathy Blvd. SW.

The neoclassical design of the Georgia state capitol, below, on Atlanta's Capitol Hill, is home to the state's legislature.

CHICAGO

Chicago's dazzling architecture and public art have turned the city into a living museum.

Great metropolises throughout the world owe their towering appearances to a prairie town where the notion of a skyscraper first came to life. Chicago possesses an architectural influence that reaches far beyond its borders: it is the birthplace of modern architecture and home to the world's first skyscraper.

The core of the city's architectural heritage is found in the Loop, bounded on the north by the Chicago River and on the south by Roosevelt Road. A sector almost synonymous with downtown Chicago, it derives its name from the two miles of elevated rapid transit track that loop around the city's bustling business district.

The first Europeans to visit the shores of Lake Michigan sensed the area's potential from the start. According to one story, in 1673 Canadian-born explorer Louis Joliet told his companion, Jacques Marquette, a Jesuit priest, "Here some day will be found one of the world's great cities."

It took almost two centuries for that prediction to come true. The first settler to arrive was fur trader Jean Baptiste Point du Sable, the son of a Quebec merchant and an African slave. In 1779

COMPETITIVE SPIRIT

COMPETITIVE SPIRIT
Chicago hosts the world's largest triathlon each August, right. As many as 4,000 athletes compete in a series of events, including the Olympic distance triathlon, which features a 1-mile swim, 25-mile bike ride, and a 6-mile run.

DISTINGUISHED LINEUP
Overleaf: Chicago claims nine of the world's tallest buildings, including the Sears Tower, the Amoco Building, and the John Hancock Center, which, at 1,127 feet, is the 10th-tallest building in the world. Opened in 1969, "Big John" was designed by the architectural firm of Skidmore, Owings and Merrill. The Sears Tower is easy to pick out of Chicago's skyline because of the building's distinctive steel cross-braces, which form huge X's on each side. From the lounge on the top floor, visitors can see parts of Illinois, Indiana, and Wisconsin.

WINDOW ON THE STREET
The rounded corner of the Carson Pirie Scott & Co. store (1899, 1903), far right, features curved windows set above arched doorways. The ironwork was painted gray for many years, but it was restored to the reddish green color intended by its creator, Louis Sullivan, as part of a much larger renovation undertaken by Chicago architect John Vinci in the 1970's.

Du Sable built a log cabin at the mouth of the Chicago River on what is today Michigan Avenue. After about 20 years he headed for Missouri, leaving behind his trading post and a handful of employees. Chicago was a frontier outpost in those days and under constant threat of Indian attack. Even when Illinois became a state in 1818, Chicago was a struggling backwater and far less populous than the southern areas of the state.

In 1829 the seeds were sown for Chicago's rise to glory. The Illinois state legislature appointed a commission to chart a canal route between Lake Michigan and the Mississippi River, and Chicago's population began to balloon. Pioneer wagons from the East Coast rolled in daily. Chicago grew from a settlement of about 50 people in 1830 to 4,000 in 1837, when it was incorporated as a city. Over the next three decades another 100,000 people arrived. Waves of Irish and German immigrants flocked here after the 100-mile canal opened and the first railroad tracks were laid in 1848.

Industry and commerce exploded with the population boom, and businessmen—not government, religious interests, or educational institutions—commissioned the first buildings. One of these was the nine-story Home Insurance Building. Designed by William Le Baron Jenney and erected in 1885, it was located at the northeast corner of LaSalle and Adams streets. Although no longer in existence, the building is remembered for its place in architectural history: it contained the first iron frame ever used. The iron frame was the forerunner of the modern steel skeleton, which supports the weight of a building and eliminates the need for thick, load-bearing walls. Jenney's work signaled the beginning of a commercial style of architecture that would be known as the Chicago School, a structural art that owed a great debt to Chicago engineers. These engineers also developed foundations that enabled the region's swampy soil to support a building's enormous weight.

THE CHICAGO SCHOOL

From the start, the Chicago School was divided into two major camps. One was spearheaded by Jenney, a strict utilitarian who sought maximum efficiency in all his buildings. He prized economy of construction, open interior space, and plenty of natural light, as demonstrated by the many bay windows on his 16-story steel-framed Manhattan Building (1891), which still stands at 431 South Dearborn Street.

The opposing faction, led by Louis Sullivan, approached architecture from a more personal and philosophical point of view. Sullivan believed that each building had a unique spirit, one that reflected its social purpose. A modern skyscraper, he once declared, "must be tall, every inch of it tall. The force and power of altitude must be in it, the glory and pride of exaltation must be in it. It must be every inch a proud and soaring thing . . . without a single dissenting line."

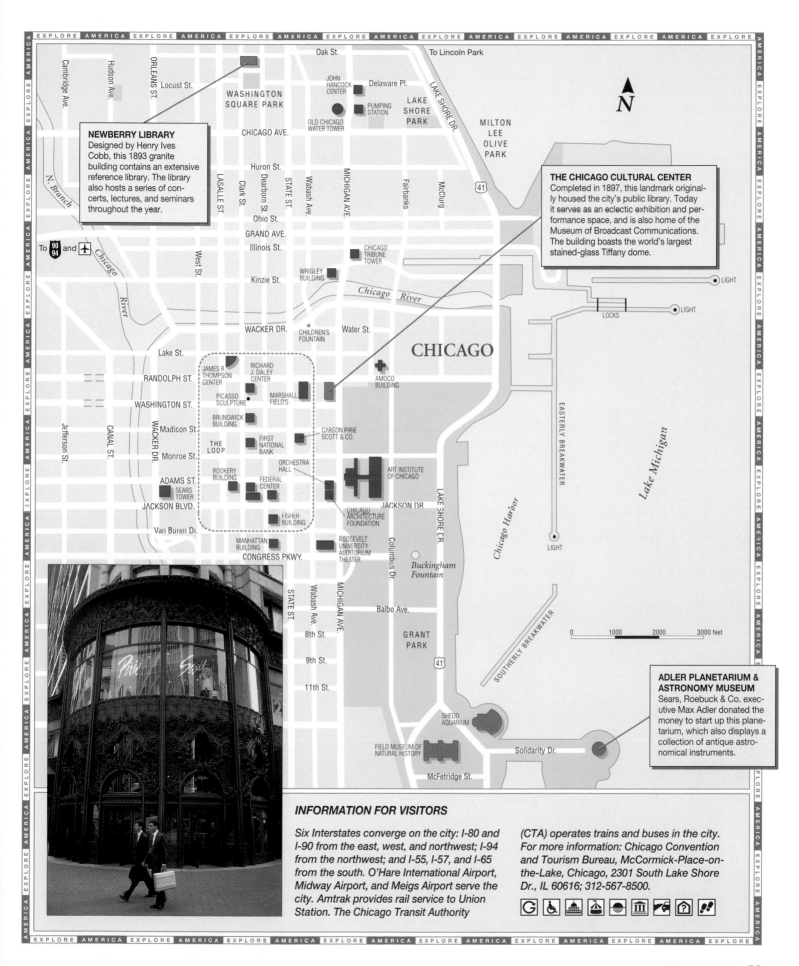

NEWBERRY LIBRARY
Designed by Henry Ives Cobb, this 1893 granite building contains an extensive reference library. The library also hosts a series of concerts, lectures, and seminars throughout the year.

THE CHICAGO CULTURAL CENTER
Completed in 1897, this landmark originally housed the city's public library. Today it serves as an eclectic exhibition and performance space, and is also home of the Museum of Broadcast Communications. The building boasts the world's largest stained-glass Tiffany dome.

ADLER PLANETARIUM & ASTRONOMY MUSEUM
Sears, Roebuck & Co. executive Max Adler donated the money to start up this planetarium, which also displays a collection of antique astronomical instruments.

CHICAGO

Oak St.
To Lincoln Park
Locust St.
ORLEANS ST.
Cambridge Ave.
Hudson Ave.
N. Branch
Chicago River
WASHINGTON SQUARE PARK
JOHN HANCOCK CENTER
Delaware Pl.
PUMPING STATION
LAKE SHORE PARK
MILTON LEE OLIVE PARK
CHICAGO AVE.
OLD CHICAGO WATER TOWER
LAKE SHORE DR.
Huron St.
LASALLE ST.
Clark St.
Dearborn St.
State St.
Wabash Ave.
MICHIGAN AVE.
Fairbanks
McClurg
Ohio St.
GRAND AVE.
West St.
Illinois St.
CHICAGO TRIBUNE TOWER
WRIGLEY BUILDING
Kinzie St.
Chicago River
WACKER DR.
CHILDREN'S FOUNTAIN
Water St.
To 90 94 and ✈
Lake St.
JAMES R. THOMPSON CENTER
RICHARD J. DALEY CENTER
RANDOLPH ST.
AMOCO BUILDING
WASHINGTON ST.
PICASSO SCULPTURE
MARSHALL FIELD'S
BRUNSWICK BUILDING
Madison St.
THE LOOP
FIRST NATIONAL BANK
CARSON PIRIE SCOTT & CO.
Monroe St.
ROOKERY BUILDING
ORCHESTRA HALL
ART INSTITUTE OF CHICAGO
ADAMS ST.
SEARS TOWER
FEDERAL CENTER
JACKSON BLVD.
JACKSON DR.
FISHER BUILDING
CHICAGO ARCHITECTURE FOUNDATION
Van Buren Dr.
Jefferson St.
CANAL ST.
WACKER DR.
MANHATTAN BUILDING
ROOSEVELT UNIVERSITY AUDITORIUM THEATER
CONGRESS PKWY.
STATE ST.
Wabash Ave.
MICHIGAN AVE.
Columbus Dr.
8th St.
9th St.
11th St.
Balbo Ave.
GRANT PARK
Buckingham Fountain
LAKE SHORE DR.
EASTERLY BREAKWATER
Lake Michigan
Chicago Harbor
LIGHT
LOCKS
LIGHT
LIGHT
SOUTHERLY BREAKWATER
LIGHT
SHEDD AQUARIUM
FIELD MUSEUM OF NATURAL HISTORY
Solidarity Dr.
McFetridge St.

0   1000   2000   3000 feet

N

INFORMATION FOR VISITORS

Six Interstates converge on the city: I-80 and I-90 from the east, west, and northwest; I-94 from the northwest; and I-55, I-57, and I-65 from the south. O'Hare International Airport, Midway Airport, and Meigs Airport serve the city. Amtrak provides rail service to Union Station. The Chicago Transit Authority (CTA) operates trains and buses in the city. For more information: Chicago Convention and Tourism Bureau, McCormick-Place-on-the-Lake, Chicago, 2301 South Lake Shore Dr., IL 60616; 312-567-8500.

EXPLORE AMERICA EXPLORE AMERICA EXPLORE AMERICA EXPLORE AMERICA EXPLORE AMERICA EXPLORE AMERICA EXPLORE AMERICA EXPLORE AMERICA EXPLORE

CHICAGO 55

The Old Chicago Water Tower, right, with the John Hancock Center looming behind it, is the only building to survive the Great Fire of 1871. The tower was built to house a 138-foot standpipe needed to equalize the pressure of water being pumped from the adjacent pumping station. Oscar Wilde, who visited Chicago in 1882, described it as a "castellated monstrosity with pepper boxes stuck all over it."

URBAN LANDSCAPE
Grant Park, below, offers a splendid view of Chicago Harbor, backed by the city's skyline.

Two of Sullivan's works, along with other landmark buildings, are included on guided tours of the Loop offered by the Chicago Architecture Foundation, which operates from its headquarters at 224 South Michigan Avenue. Sullivan's Auditorium Building (1887–89) on Michigan Avenue was conceived in partnership with German-born Dankmar Adler, who provided the engineering prowess, while Sullivan played the dual roles of artist and planner. The building is divided along horizontal lines rather than vertical ones, beginning with a base made of rusticated granite, followed by a midsection of smooth limestone, and topped with a floor marked by small windows in groups of three. Although the structure originally was designed for offices, a hotel, and a theater, it now houses the downtown campus of Roosevelt University and the Auditorium Theater, one of the finest performance spaces in the city. During World War II the stage was converted into a bowling alley before being carefully restored in the 1960's.

CROONER'S FAVORITE

A stroll to State Street—"that Great Street" in Frank Sinatra's popular song of 1957 titled "Chicago"—displays Sullivan's penchant for ornamentation. Especially notable is the grillwork on the Carson Pirie Scott & Co. department store, opened in 1899. The ornamentation was criticized at the time as being too elaborate for a commercial building. But Sullivan believed that display windows merited rich frames.

Branching out from State Street the city becomes a veritable garden of public art—and has been

ever since 1967, when a gigantic untitled work by Pablo Picasso was erected outside the 31-story Richard J. Daley Center, located within the Loop.

As the story goes, architect William E. Hartmann persuaded Picasso to design a work for Chicago—a city the artist had never visited—by plying him with gifts: a photograph album of Chicago's most famous residents, including Ernest Hemingway (a friend of Picasso's); a helmet worn by the fire chief; and the uniforms of the Bears and the White Sox, two of Chicago's major league sports teams. Apparently impressed with the offerings, Picasso gave the city his work of art at no cost—a 50-foot-tall, 162-ton steel sculpture that still provokes viewers to ask, "What is it?" Some say the sculpture resembles a dog, others say a bird. In actual fact, the sculpture represents the head of a woman.

No such puzzle exists outside the First National Bank, where Russian artist Marc Chagall's monolith, weighing 4,000 tons, covers 3,000 square feet at the base of the 850-foot-high bank. Titled *The Four Seasons* (1974), Chagall's work is a mosaic of fanciful scenes of Chicago life created with inlaid brick and tiny chips of glass in more than 250 shades of color. Chagall was clear about his design. "I chose the subject of the four seasons," he said, "because I felt this represents the four seasons of all of life and of life itself."

Although there isn't any mystery surrounding *Miró's Chicago* (1981), Joan Miró's steel, bronze, and cement sculpture of a woman sometimes provokes a powerful response. Several weeks after the large, rounded form was dedicated on a site adjacent to the 38-story Brunswick Building, a machinist threw a quart of red paint on the artwork. He later explained to authorities that he simply didn't like the sculpture.

A far warmer welcome signaled the installation of Alexander Calder's red stabile. Accompanied by a circus parade, Calder rode into the Loop on a wagon pulled by 40 horses the day *Flamingo* was dedicated in 1974. The abstract sculpture—which Calder said was "sort of pink and has a long neck"—provides a free-flowing contrast to the disciplined lines of the three buildings that make up the adjacent Federal Center (1959).

EUROPEAN INFLUENCE

The Federal Center is considered one of the finest works of architect Ludwig Mies van der Rohe, who left Germany in 1937 when it became clear to him that his modernist International Style would never be accepted by the Nazis. The complex is distinguished by the architect's spare geometry and dark steel and glass curtain walls. Mies van der Rohe's philosophy—"less is more"—influenced an entire generation of

WHIMSY FROM THE TWENTIES
The corner clock, above, was a fanciful addition to the terra-cotta high-rise at 35 East Wacker Drive. The structure was once called the Jewelers Building (1926) because it housed numerous jewelry firms. Originally tenants could drive their cars into the building, steer them onto the elevator, and ride up to their designated parking spaces on one of the lower 22 floors.

ENIGMATIC GAZE
The untitled sculpture, left, at the Richard J. Daley Center has become known to Chicagoans as simply "the Picasso." Made of Cor-Ten steel and standing 50 feet high, this abstract piece of art depicts the head of a woman. It was the first monumental piece of modern art in the city's public art collection, which consists of almost 100 works. The pieces are scattered between the banks of the Chicago River to the north and the Field Museum of Natural History to the south.

*The Children's Fountain (1983),
right, at Wacker Drive and Wabash
Avenue was conceived as an embodiment
of the spirit of Daniel
Burnham's Chicago Plan of 1909.
Beyond it stands the ornate steel-
framed Wrigley Building (1924),
designed on orders from the wealthy
chewing-gum magnate to resemble
a luscious birthday cake. The
Tribune Tower (1925), to the right,
displays Gothic elements that pro-
voked criticism from some contemporary architects, who believed
that modern skyscrapers ought
not borrow from bygone eras.*

MASTERS' WORK

*The court of the Rookery Building,
below, was restored in 1992.
Designed by the architectural firm
Burnham & Root and built between
1885 and 1888, the structure wraps
around an interior court and is
roofed by a skylight. In 1905 the
court was remodeled by Frank
Lloyd Wright—one of Chicago's
most famous residents—who paid
particular attention to the ornamentation of gold and ivory.*

architects whose stark structuralism distinguishes
soaring, unadorned skyscrapers not only in
Chicago, but also in other cities across the country.

THE WINDY CITY

Chicago's outdoor art does not
overshadow the fine art found
behind closed doors. At the
Art Institute of Chicago, on
Michigan Avenue, visitors can savor everything
from windows designed by legendary architect
Frank Lloyd Wright and salvaged from buildings
slated for destruction to the largest collection
of Impressionist paintings outside the Louvre in
Paris, France. The building, erected in 1893, was
originally constructed as an office space for international participants in the World's Columbian
Exposition in 1893—a fair that led to Chicago's
being dubbed the Windy City, a name that, oddly
enough, has nothing to do with the weather. When

Chicago was vying to host the fair, its chief rival was New York City. *New York Sun* editor Charles Dana portrayed Chicagoans as braggarts and told his readers to pay no attention to "the nonsensical claims of that windy city."

Architecturally, the 1893 World's Columbian Exposition proved a turning point for the city, convincing those in power that Chicago needed a detailed plan to avoid urban sprawl. Daniel H. Burnham, the exposition's principal designer, was engaged to develop the 1909 Chicago Plan, considered the most influential urban planning document ever produced. Burnham designed a variety of structures that still stand, including the Fisher Building (1896) on South Dearborn Street, which applies Gothic ornamentation to a turn-of-the-century skyscraper, and the neo-Georgian Orchestra Hall (1905) on South Michigan Avenue.

Chicago's commercial architecture has been grandly compared to that of Baroque Rome, and certainly the best of the metropolis' buildings possess more than their fair share of splendor. While many of Chicago's finest buildings have been torn down over the years and replaced with parking lots or nondescript office towers, recently the city has begun to cultivate renewed pride in its architectural heritage. As restoration and renovation become common practice, Chicago's extraordinary collection of buildings will survive to greet 21st-century visitors to this glittering city.

DIZZYING VIEW
The James R. Thompson Center, left, designed by architect Helmut Jahn, curls around a dazzling atrium that is 17 stories high. The massive glass-and-granite building houses 50 departments of state government, an Illinois artisans shop, and a large food court. It is named after the Illinois governor who selected Jahn's design in 1985.

MAGICAL DRIVE
Lake Shore Drive winds through Lincoln Park, left, part of the 29 miles of Lake Michigan's shoreline protected by the city's park system.

OTHER SITES & ATTRACTIONS

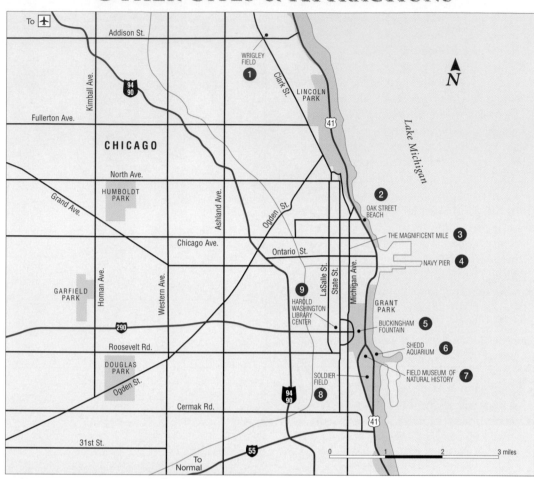

Visitors enjoy a balmy summer day by sunbathing on Oak Street Beach and wading in the chilly waters of Lake Michigan, below.

❶ WRIGLEY FIELD

Built in 1914 and home to the Chicago Cubs, Wrigley Field is a reminder of how baseball used to be played. With its ivy-covered walls, manually operated scoreboard, and contingent of loyal fans, a trip to the stadium is like stepping back in time. Located at 1060 W. Addison St.

❷ OAK STREET BEACH

Oak Street Beach draws joggers, bikers, skate-boarders, and strollers of every age to the water's edge. Swimming and wading are also popular, although the lake can be chilly even in August. Located where Oak St. meets Lake Michigan.

❸ THE MAGNIFICENT MILE

North Michigan Ave. is Chicago's Fifth Ave., home to many of the city's upscale retail stores, including Bloomingdale's, Polo Ralph Lauren, and Giacomo. The centerpiece is a vertical mall called Water Tower Place, which takes its name from the limestone water tower across the street, one of the few structures to survive the Great Fire of Chicago in 1871. The mall features a Lord & Taylor department store,

seven levels of specialty stores, and a different department of Marshall Field's on every floor. Located between the Chicago River and Oak St.

4 NAVY PIER

Patterned on Ghirardelli Square in San Francisco, this renovated pier juts into Lake Michigan and supports more than 50 acres of parks, gardens, shops, and restaurants. The Chicago Children's Museum, a $14.5-million, 57,000-square-foot building with interactive exhibits on subjects ranging from garbage collection to racial prejudice, is popular with young visitors. Located at 700 E. Grand Ave.

5 BUCKINGHAM FOUNTAIN

Perhaps Chicago's most photographed tourist attraction, this pink Georgia marble fountain built in 1927 is patterned on one at Louis XIV's palace at Versailles, France—but at twice the size. Four pairs of bronze sea horses adorn the base of the fountain. On summer evenings computers coordinate the flow of water that spouts from its 133 jets, as well as the beams from hundreds of spotlights. Located inside Grant Park.

6 SHEDD AQUARIUM

Named after its benefactor, John G. Shedd, this huge aquarium houses more than 8,000 aquatic animals, making it the world's largest indoor collection of marine life. The Shedd's leading attraction is the Oceanarium, a 3-million-gallon glass tank that holds whales, seals, dolphins, and penguins, and is designed so that it appears to be in the middle of Lake Michigan. Located at 1200 S. Lake Shore Dr.

7 FIELD MUSEUM OF NATURAL HISTORY

Patterned on an ancient Greek temple, this enormous building displays outstanding permanent exhibits that include dinosaur skeletons, stuffed elephants, a pharaoh's tomb, a collection of art

by Pacific Coast peoples, and precious jewelry created by Louis Comfort Tiffany. Located on Roosevelt Rd. at Lake Shore Dr.

8 SOLDIER FIELD

A U-shaped stadium supported by Doric columns, Soldier Field recalls the grandeur of ancient Greece. Its design complements that of the Field Museum, which is located nearby. Soldier Field, erected between 1922 and 1926 and home to the Chicago Bears, was named in memory of the soldiers who fought in World War I. The roofless football stadium and Chicago's chilly winter climate helped the Bears gain a reputation for toughness in the National Football League. Located at 425 S. McFetridge Dr.

9 HAROLD WASHINGTON LIBRARY CENTER

The Chicago Public Library's Harold Washington Library Center, named for the city's first African-American mayor, opened in 1991. The largest municipal library in the nation, it was built at a cost of $144 million and houses some 1.7 million books and 12,500 periodicals. Located at 400 S. State St.

SANTA FE

*A meeting place of histories
and cultures, Santa Fe
is a magical town.*

In the coolness brought by a sudden afternoon downpour, Pueblo Indians sit wrapped in blankets under the portal of the Palace of the Governors. Eager tourists, umbrellas in hand, crowd under the porch roof, eyeing the jewelry and pottery spread out on the damp sidewalk. Young Hispanic men rub raindrops off their finely restored automobiles, which are lined up around the plaza like beauty contestants. A mounted policeman in a yellow slicker clip-clops around the block on a horse. It's Friday afternoon in Santa Fe, New Mexico, and this lively scene is a continuation of the long procession of this city's colorful culture and history.

The oldest state capital in the country, Santa Fe has been called the City Different, and with good reason. At first view the most distinctive difference is its architecture. Many structures are made of adobe, a steadfast reminder of Santa Fe's Spanish and Puebloan heritage. The earthen colors of adobe are complemented by hand-hewn wooden beams. The buildings are low-slung, their porches and balconies hung with strings of red chili *ristras*. Carved doors and gates are often

intricately sculptured artwork. Sidewalks dogleg through the city, and small courtyards and gardens overflow with columbines, irises, and roses. This is a city for walkers and for those who wish to avoid the noise and crowds so common in most major metropolises. There are no honking horns and precious little hustle and bustle. This is not a city of canyons of concrete, steel, and glass. Rather, Santa Fe, nestled in the foothills of the Sangre de Cristo Mountains, remains the land of mañana.

SETTLEMENT AND REVOLT

More than seven centuries ago the ancestors of modern-day Pueblo Indians built villages north and south of Santa Fe along the Rio Grande: San Ildefonso, Santa Clara, Santo Domingo, Nambé, and Tesuque, among others. Here they cultivated corn, beans, squash, and chilies in the fertile fields beside the river. They still maintain strong ties to their native culture and traditions, and a visit to a summer or winter ceremony at one of these outlying pueblos, or villages, is a popular excursion for visitors.

In 1607 Spanish colonists founded Santa Fe on a tributary of the Rio Grande. The settlement was originally called La Villa Real de la Santa Fé de San Francisco de Asís, or the Royal City of Holy Faith of St. Francis of Assisi. Santa Fe's early inhabitants, mostly missionaries looking to convert the indigenous population to Christianity, soon discovered that this rough-edged outpost on New Spain's

northern frontier was unforgiving. Isolation, drought, smallpox epidemics, and Indian raids were just some of the early hardships faced by the colonists. As author Bill Jamison observes in his book *The Insider's Guide to Santa Fe*, the city "yielded little gold or glory and the native population took to God only in limited and frustrating ways."

Under the orders of New Mexico's governor, Don Pedro de Peralta, the Palace of the Governors was built in 1610. The low, block-long adobe building was a palace in name only. The floors were made of dirt, and the roof, made of logs grouted with mud, reportedly always leaked. Over the years the original adobe structure was remodeled several times; a Victorian-style balustrade was added in 1877, and the palace was restored in the Spanish–Pueblo Revival style between 1909 and 1910. The palace, the oldest existing public building in the nation, now serves as one of five museums operated by the State History Museum for New Mexico. The rooms are filled with some 17,000 historic artifacts chronicling New Mexico's rich history. Of particular interest are the Plexiglas openings in the floor and walls, which allow amateur archeologists to gaze upon the foundation and other fascinating relics that date back to the 17th century.

In 1680 the Pueblo Indians revolted against Spanish rule and laid siege to the 1,000 settlers who had sought refuge in the courtyard. The colonists held out until their water supply was severed, then retreated 300 miles to the south. The Indians

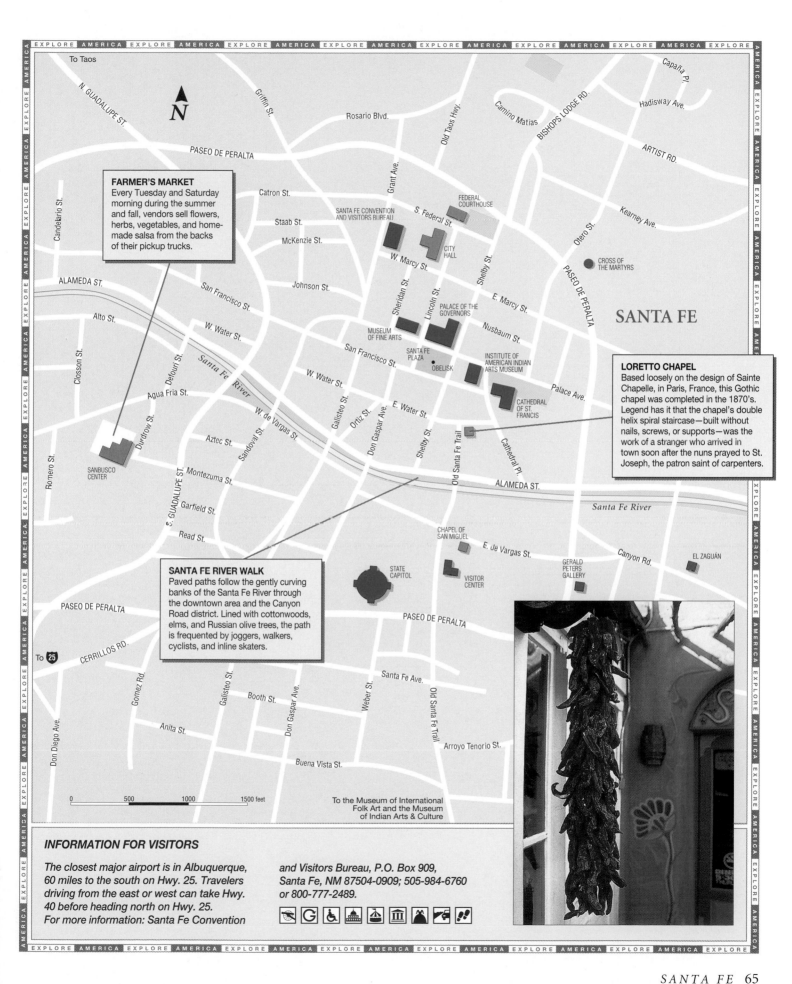

To Taos

N. GUADALUPE ST.

Griffin St.

Rosario Blvd.

Capaña Pl.

Hadisway Ave.

PASEO DE PERALTA

Old Taos Hwy.

Camino Matias

BISHOPS LODGE RD.

ARTIST RD.

Grant Ave.

Catron St.

FARMER'S MARKET
Every Tuesday and Saturday morning during the summer and fall, vendors sell flowers, herbs, vegetables, and home-made salsa from the backs of their pickup trucks.

Candelario St.

Staab St.

McKenzie St.

SANTA FE CONVENTION AND VISITORS BUREAU

S. Federal St.

FEDERAL COURTHOUSE

Kearney Ave.

W. Marcy St.

CITY HALL

Shelby St.

Otero St.

PASEO DE PERALTA

CROSS OF THE MARTYRS

ALAMEDA ST.

San Francisco St.

Johnson St.

Sheridan St.

Lincoln St.

E. Marcy St.

SANTA FE

Alto St.

W. Water St.

PALACE OF THE GOVERNORS

Nusbaum St.

Closson St.

Santa Fe River

MUSEUM OF FINE ARTS

SANTA FE PLAZA

OBELISK

INSTITUTE OF AMERICAN INDIAN ARTS MUSEUM

LORETTO CHAPEL
Based loosely on the design of Sainte Chapelle, in Paris, France, this Gothic chapel was completed in the 1870's. Legend has it that the chapel's double helix spiral staircase—built without nails, screws, or supports—was the work of a stranger who arrived in town soon after the nuns prayed to St. Joseph, the patron saint of carpenters.

Agua Fria St.

Defouri St.

W. Water St.

San Francisco St.

Galisteo St.

Ortiz St.

E. Water St.

Don Gaspar Ave.

Shelby St.

Palace Ave.

CATHEDRAL OF ST. FRANCIS

Cathedral Pl.

Old Santa Fe Trail

Durdrow St.

SANBUSCO CENTER

Aztec St.

Sandoval St.

S. GUADALUPE ST.

Montezuma St.

ALAMEDA ST.

Santa Fe River

Romero St.

Garfield St.

Read St.

SANTA FE RIVER WALK
Paved paths follow the gently curving banks of the Santa Fe River through the downtown area and the Canyon Road district. Lined with cottonwoods, elms, and Russian olive trees, the path is frequented by joggers, walkers, cyclists, and inline skaters.

CHAPEL OF SAN MIGUEL

E. De Vargas St.

Canyon Rd.

GERALD PETERS GALLERY

EL ZAGUÁN

STATE CAPITOL

VISITOR CENTER

PASEO DE PERALTA

PASEO DE PERALTA

CERRILLOS RD.

To 25

Gomez Rd.

Galisteo St.

Booth St.

Weber St.

Santa Fe Ave.

Old Santa Fe Trail

Don Diego Ave.

Anita St.

Don Gaspar Ave.

Arroyo Tenorio St.

Buena Vista St.

0   500   1000   1500 feet

To the Museum of International Folk Art and the Museum of Indian Arts & Culture

INFORMATION FOR VISITORS

The closest major airport is in Albuquerque, 60 miles to the south on Hwy. 25. Travelers driving from the east or west can take Hwy. 40 before heading north on Hwy. 25.
For more information: Santa Fe Convention and Visitors Bureau, P.O. Box 909, Santa Fe, NM 87504-0909; 505-984-6760 or 800-777-2489.

EXPLORE AMERICA EXPLORE AMERICA EXPLORE AMERICA EXPLORE AMERICA EXPLORE AMERICA EXPLORE AMERICA EXPLORE AMERICA EXPLORE AMERICA EXPLORE AMERICA EXPLORE

SANTA FE 65

converted the palace into a pueblo and occupied it until 1692, when Spanish forces under the command of Don Diego de Vargas reclaimed it.

Every year since 1712, the five-day celebration of Las Fiestas de Santa Fé, usually following Labor Day, has commemorated the Spanish recapture of the city. Festival highlights include the burning in effigy of Zozobra (a mythical figure representing gloom), parades, and traditional Spanish dances and songs. The celebration ends with a mass. Many of the festivities take place in the tree-lined Santa Fe Plaza, just across from the palace.

TRAFFIC FROM THE EAST

Situated in the heart of Santa Fe, the Santa Fe Plaza has been the stage upon which the city's tumultuous history has been played out through four centuries. Originally laid out by the Spanish colonists as a military parade ground, the rectangular open-air plaza has been used for everything from political rallies and religious processions to bullfights and public floggings.

Most significantly, the spacious plaza is located at the end of the famed Santa Fe Trail. When Mexico gained its independence from Spain in 1821, Santa Fe was named the capital of its province of New Mexico. That same year, explorer William Becknell led 21 men and a pack train of goods from Franklin, Missouri, some 1,000 miles to Santa Fe—opening the Santa Fe Trail and spurring five days of celebration in the plaza. The establishment of the trail opened the previously unexploited territory to American merchants from the East. Santa Fe became the hub of mercantile activity and was soon bustling with brawny wagon masters and a colorful array of traders, who quickly transformed the plaza into a raucous meeting place.

Open borders with Mexico ignited American interest in the area. In 1846, at the outset of the Mexican War, Gen. Stephen Watts Kearny led the Army of the West into the Mexican town of Las Vegas, and claimed the area for the United States. Kearny then headed to Santa Fe where, preparing for a counteroffensive by Mexican troops, he began the construction of Fort Marcy. The attack never materialized and, with the signing of the Treaty of Guadalupe Hidalgo in 1848, New Mexico officially became a territory of the United States.

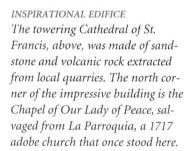

INSPIRATIONAL EDIFICE
The towering Cathedral of St. Francis, above, was made of sandstone and volcanic rock extracted from local quarries. The north corner of the impressive building is the Chapel of Our Lady of Peace, salvaged from La Parroquia, a 1717 adobe church that once stood here.

DISTINCTIVE ARCHITECTURE
Much of Santa Fe's charm stems from its distinctly Southwestern architecture. The small house on Canyon Road, opposite page, displays the fluid lines and irregular shapes typical of adobe dwellings. Thick walls and small windows help keep the heat out. Elsewhere in town, a trading post storefront, left, tempts shoppers with everything from pottery and paintings to beadwork and baskets.

STATELY INTERIOR
Inside the state capitol, below,
cleaner lines prevail. Also known as
the Roundhouse, its shape was pat-
terned after a Zia Indian sun sym-
bol. The capitol contains galleries
that display works by local artists.

But as much as Santa Fe cherishes its public spaces, the city worships its religious places. The showpiece is the Cathedral of St. Francis, located one block from the plaza. This structure of limestone and light volcanic rock was designed in the Romanesque style under the eye of Bishop Jean Baptiste Lamy, who is buried in a crypt beneath the sanctuary. In 1851 Bishop Lamy arrived in Santa Fe and quickly infused the city with his energy, ideas, and organization. Work began on the church in 1869 and took 17 years to complete. Entering the church today, visitors are likely to see worshipers kneeling in prayer, many of them women wearing lace mantillas on their heads. Stained-glass windows diffuse soft light throughout the nave. In the North Transept a wooden statue of the Virgin, *La Conquistadora*—first brought to Santa Fe in 1625—gazes solemnly upon visitors.

CREATIVE COMMUNITY Santa Fe's diverse cultural history, dramatic natural surroundings, and close ties to Native American spirituality have long made it a haven for artists. As early as 1910, with the arrival of painters Robert Henri and John Sloan, the city began attracting many of the country's preeminent young writers and artists. Included among this immigration of creative talents were *Los Cinco Pintores,* or "The Five Painters": Jozef Bakos, Fremont Ellis, Walter Mruk, Willard Nash, and Will Shuster. By 1921 their works were being shown collectively at the Museum of Fine Arts. The museum, located next to the Palace of the Governors, is one of the few institutions in the country that was founded by local artists in order to exhibit their own works.

MODEL MUSEUM
The exterior of the Museum of Fine Arts, left, was modeled on the New Mexico building at the 1915–16 Panama-California Exposition in San Diego. Many of its architectural features, such as the hand-hewn crossbeams and ceilings of split cedar, were influenced by those of Spanish mission churches.

ART AROUND EVERY CORNER
Native American craftspeople display beautiful turquoise jewelry, below. Local vendors congregate at the Palace of the Governors and the Santa Fe Plaza, where they sell everything from traditional jewelry and kachina dolls to brightly colored textiles and paintings.

Today the museum displays a selection of its 7,000 pieces of regional art dating back to the late 19th century. Among the highlights of the collection are works by pioneering resident artist Georgia O'Keeffe, The Five Painters, and Bert Geer Phillips and Ernest L. Blumenschein, both of whom came to the region by wagon in 1898.

Two other renowned museums are situated along the Old Santa Fe Trail. The Museum of International Folk Art is popular with visitors young and old who delight in viewing whimsical pieces of folk art from all over the world. Displays include dolls and dollhouses, plaques, ornaments, tin retablos, paper cutouts, African puppets, and entire village scenes that have been replicated in miniature form.

Across the way Native American history and culture is celebrated at the Museum of Indian Arts & Culture. Detailed displays range from prehistoric times to the present, giving visitors a sense of the rich history of the region's indigenous peoples. Among the items on display are ancient cooking utensils, Clovis arrowheads, and a 150-foot-long hunting net woven out of human hair.

Santa Fe itself is an artwork in progress. Travelers who take a stroll up Canyon Road will see examples

ANCIENT HOUSE OF WORSHIP
The interior of the Chapel of San Miguel, above, reflects the various cultures of the region: New Mexican dried chilies hang next to European religious icons. Originally built in 1610, the chapel roof was burned during the Pueblo Revolt of 1680. It was restored in 1693 and remodeled and enlarged in 1710.

The best way to experience the magic of Santa Fe is on foot. Chilies hang from doorways and the smell of frijoles and tortillas makes mouths water. On Christmas Eve the city bathes in the flickering glow of *farolitos*—votive candles in paper bags that are placed in windows and along walls and awnings. In the spring and summer the same streets are adorned with the colors and sweet scents of blooming wildflowers.

The mixture of the New and Old worlds is evident throughout the city. Inside the Chapel of San Miguel, built in 1610 and reputedly the country's oldest Christian church in continuous use, visitors can examine biblical scenes that were painted on animal skins by the Spanish missionaries in order to teach Christianity to the Pueblo Indians.

Like all prosperous cities, Santa Fe has experienced its share of growing pains. Longtime residents bemoan the changes—too much fake adobe, too many hand-tooled ostrich cowboy boots, too much high-priced real estate. But changes have been taking place here for almost 400 years, and it is precisely this dialogue between the past and present that gives Santa Fe such a dynamic future.

of the diversity of art that makes the city one of the country's most vibrant centers of creativity. Some 80 galleries are strung out along less than a mile of this narrow street. They display contemporary and traditional paintings, jewelry, glass, metal, textiles, and works made of neon. Numerous temporary galleries open during the summer. Art buyers and serious collectors never miss the city's two biggest annual art markets—Indian Market, the third weekend in August, and Spanish Market, which takes place the last weekend in July.

Called the "art and soul of Santa Fe," Canyon Road is a wonderful mixture of art, literature, and architecture. The Gerald Peters Gallery, a few blocks off Canyon Road, was once La Casa Querida, a house built in 1925 by author Mary Austin. A lush wisteria vine she planted still cloaks the patio wall. Farther down the road stands El Zaguán hacienda. Bought by merchant James Johnson in the mid-1800's, the 300-foot-long house underwent many changes until the Historic Santa Fe Foundation acquired it in 1979. El Zaguán's garden, a special Santa Fe sanctuary, is shaded by a huge horse chestnut tree and planted with roses, delphiniums, and peonies originally imported from China. Today the hacienda houses private apartments.

POPULAR PLAZA
Pedestrians stroll through the Santa Fe Plaza, above, while others sit at the edge of an obelisk that commemorates New Mexicans who fought in the Indian and Civil wars. The plaza, which is the heart of Santa Fe, hosts a variety of concerts and events throughout the year.

PRESERVING CULTURES
The graceful lines of the Museum of Indian Arts & Culture, left, are inspired by traditional pueblo architecture. The museum's collection includes more than 100,000 art objects made by Native Americans of the region.

OTHER SITES & ATTRACTIONS

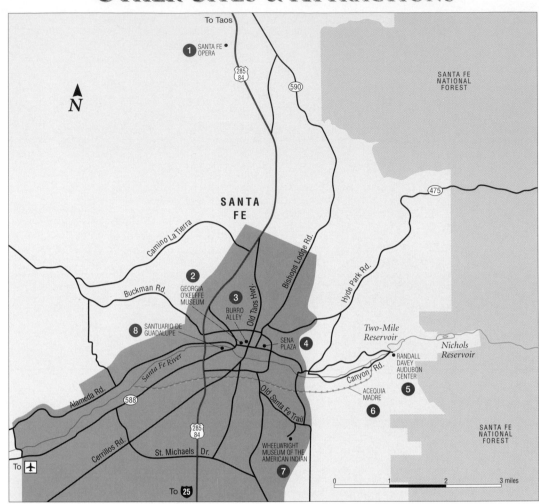

A bronze sculpture titled Heading Home, *below, stands outside the Wheelwright Museum of the American Indian. Created by Apache sculptor Allan Houser, the work depicts a traditional Navajo goatherd tending her flock.*

1 SANTA FE OPERA

Every summer for more than 40 years, people have come to see and hear world-class productions of *La Traviata, La Boheme,* and other operas performed at this open-air venue. Some in the audience at this most casual of opera houses feel comfortable wearing blue jeans and cowboy boots, while others prefer the more formal attire of black ties and tuxedos. Seasoned operagoers often start the evening with a tailgate picnic of champagne and caviar. The opera house, once open to the night sky, is now roofed to protect the audience and performers from summer thunderstorms. But the building's open sides still offer outstanding views of the surrounding terrain. Located seven miles north of Santa Fe on Hwys. 285 and 84.

2 GEORGIA O'KEEFFE MUSEUM

The Georgia O'Keeffe Museum, which opened in July 1997, is the latest addition to Santa Fe's illustrious family of museums. O'Keeffe was born on a farm in Sun Prairie, Wisconsin, and studied art in Chicago and New York before she visited New Mexico and decided to move here in 1949 after the death of her husband, photographer Alfred Stieglitz. The

museum's 10 galleries display more than 80 of O'Keeffe's singular works—the largest permanent collection of her art in the world. Most of the paintings, including many of her famous close-up oil paintings of flowers, were donated by private collectors after plans for the museum were officially announced. The museum is housed in a historic church at 217 Johnson St. in Santa Fe.

③ BURRO ALLEY

This tiny pathway received its name because woodcutters once hitched their burros here. These pack animals were laden with piñon pine and juniper wood brought down from the mountains to be offered for sale in town. To keep the burros from being frightened by pedestrian traffic, their owners covered the animals' eyes. When business was slow, the woodcutters would while away the time in the nearest cantina. On cold days, the fragrant piñon pine, burning in adobe fireplaces, still sweetens the air of Santa Fe. Located between West San Francisco St. and West Palace Ave. in the downtown area.

④ SENA PLAZA

The courtyard of Sena Plaza entices visitors to stop and admire the columbines and roses that flourish here. This secluded plaza was once the central courtyard of a 33-room adobe hacienda that was built in the 1860's and belonged to Maj. Don José and Dona Isabel Sena. The hacienda's spacious ballroom was used as the legislative assembly after the territorial capitol was devastated by fire in 1892. A few small shops and a restaurant with an outdoor terrace face the courtyard. Located just east of Santa Fe Plaza on Palace Ave.

⑤ RANDALL DAVEY AUDUBON CENTER

This 135-acre wildlife sanctuary allows visitors to enjoy the beautiful natural surroundings of Santa Fe. The half-mile El Temporal Nature Trail winds through sagebrush meadows and piñon-juniper woods. Among the many species of birds that frequent the area are hummingbirds, swallows, northern flickers, ravens, and mountain chickadees. Buildings at the center include a farm and a sawmill that served as home and studio for local artist Randall Davey. A pair of magnificent century-old cottonwoods shade the buildings. Located at the end of Upper Canyon Rd.

  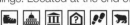

⑥ ACEQUIA MADRE

The *Acequia Madre*, or "Mother Ditch," is an irrigation canal that courses through Santa Fe along the street of the same name. Irrigation systems, developed in Spain while it was under Moorish rule, were introduced into New Mexico by Hispanic agriculturists in the 1600's. Water was diverted from the nearest stream—in this case the Santa Fe River—and into the *acequia madre*. From here the water was distributed into smaller ditches, known as *sangrias*,

which carried the water to individual plots of land. Any excess water was funneled back into the mother ditch and used downstream. When Santa Fe was laid out in 1610, there were two *acequias madres*, one on the south side and one on the north side of the river. The northern one was renamed, while the one on the south became the official acequia madre. Located in Santa Fe.

⑦ WHEELWRIGHT MUSEUM OF THE AMERICAN INDIAN

One of three museums off the Old Santa Fe Trail, the Wheelwright was founded in 1937 by Mary Cabot Wheelwright to help preserve the culture of the Navajo people. Working with a Navajo medicine man named Hastiin Klah, Wheelwright designed the museum in the shape of a traditional Navajo home, or hogan. The museum houses an extensive collection of historic and contemporary Native American artwork. The museum shop, a replica of a Navajo trading post, offers an excellent selection of Native American arts and crafts. Located in the Camino Lejo Museum Complex in Santa Fe.

⑧ SANTUARIO DE GUADALUPE

Built by Franciscan monks between 1776 and 1796, the Santuario de Guadalupe is the country's oldest shrine to Our Lady of Guadalupe. Constructed of adobe in the Mexican parish style, the original structure had a dirt floor and no pews; members of the choir had to climb a ladder to reach the loft. The church was not used on a regular basis until the 1880's, when Father James DeFouri oversaw extensive renovations. Remodeling the dilapidated structure after New England–style churches, DeFouri replaced the flat roof with a pitched one and added a white picket fence. Much of the church was destroyed by fire in 1922, forcing another spate of reconstruction. Today visitors can see remnants of the charred roof in the archway of the entrance to the Meditation Chapel. A beautiful reredos, or altar painting, featuring the Virgin of Guadalupe survived the fire. It dates to 1783 and was brought by oxcart from Mexico. The shrine is maintained as a public art center by the Guadalupe Historic Foundation, and it continues to hold a church service weekly. Located near the end of Camino Real.

Visitors to the Randall Davey Audubon Center, above, tour the grounds. The center's half-mile loop trail connects with another path that extends beyond the grounds and into Santa Fe Canyon.

During repairs to the bell tower of the Santuario de Guadalupe, below, in 1989, the remains of more than 80 young women believed killed by an epidemic at the end of the 19th century were found beneath the floor. The remains are now contained in a special crypt.

SALT LAKE CITY

Once an isolated Mormon refuge, this city is now a thriving cultural and commercial center.

Most American cities celebrate their past, but few do so with the fervor of Salt Lake City. Unlike other pioneer settlements, the city is located neither at a natural crossroads, a railroad junction, nor at the mouth of a river. It didn't begin with a lone trapper wandering into the valley and erecting a log cabin beside a stream. And the city did not burst into existence overnight as did Denver, Colorado, when gold was discovered along Cherry Creek. Utah's Salt Lake City grew out of a religious vision experienced by Brigham Young, the successor to Joseph Smith as the leader of the Mormons, who took his followers away from persecution in search of refuge. He found such a place on the shore of a salt-saturated sea in the middle of the Great American Desert.

The defining moment in the Mormons' quest occurred in 1847 when they arrived at the mouth of Emigration Canyon, overlooking the Salt Lake valley. Brigham Young took in the broad view and announced to his group: "It is enough. This is the right place."

SPRINGTIME VIEW
Overleaf: Yellow clover flourishes on the hills overlooking Salt Lake City.

'TIS THE SEASON
The Christmas season in Temple Square, below, is celebrated with a life-size Nativity scene, movies, concerts, and some 300,000 Christmas lights strung on trees, bushes, and buildings, including the Temple.

It is fortunate that the Mormons, or Latter-day Saints (LDS) as they call themselves, halted their journey where they did, for beyond the Great Salt Lake lies some of the most implacable desert on earth. Had the immigrants continued westward, they might never have succeeded in realizing their dream. As history has since shown, the conditions between Utah and the Pacific Coast for a city based on agriculture are not favorable. And while California and Oregon provided opportunities, Young had ruled these out as being overpopulated. The Mormons wanted independence of the sort they could have only through isolation; they sought a place that no one else wanted. It is truly remarkable, considering how little was known at the time about this region, that they chose one of the few areas that could support the kind of society they hoped to create.

The place where Young stood is marked today by an impressive granite memorial in This Is the Place State Park. The 60-foot-high monument, which pays tribute to the white explorers and settlers of the region, was created by Mahonri Young, Brigham's grandson. The figure of Brigham Young himself stands atop the granite tower, flanked by two other church presidents, Heber C. Kimball and Wilford Woodruff. Nearby stands Old Deseret, a reconstructed pioneer village dominated by the Brigham Young Forest Farmhouse, which was built by the Mormon leader. Visitors to the park, until recently known as Pioneer Trail State Park, begin to appreciate what those 19th-century pioneers accomplished in taming the terrain. To the east of the city, the Wasatch Range rises in a smooth rampart to 11,500 feet and more. To the west unfolds a spectacular, and daunting, vista that takes in the vast and shimmering waters of Great Salt Lake, the Oquirrh Mountains, and the desert beyond.

NEW BEGINNING

The first party of Mormons—148 people traveling in 72 wagons—was an advance team. Behind them, approximately 1,500 members of their sect, known formally as the Church of the Latter-day Saints, were strung out across a thousand miles of open country, working their way across the continent. During the next 20 years, some 70,000 more people made their way to this little-known valley on the far side of the Rocky Mountains. Some of the pioneers arrived with plentiful supplies, whereas others staggered in on foot with scarcely more than the clothes on their backs. Most were lifelong Mormons who, after years of hostility, had abandoned their homes in Ohio, Missouri, and Illinois to head west. A few had seen their leader and prophet, Joseph Smith, murdered by a mob. There were recent converts among their numbers, many of them Europeans who were also fleeing limited prospects and grinding poverty in their homelands overseas.

It was the task of the first settlers to prepare the land for those who followed. They planted a field of potatoes, diverting water from a nearby creek to irrigate it. Before the ground for the first house was leveled, Young marked the center of the city grid, the future site of the Temple. The design was carefully laid out in accordance to Mormon scripture: it would "lieth four-square, and in length as great as the breadth." The plan was eminently logical. Every address in Salt Lake City is numbered from the meridian marker on the southeast cor-

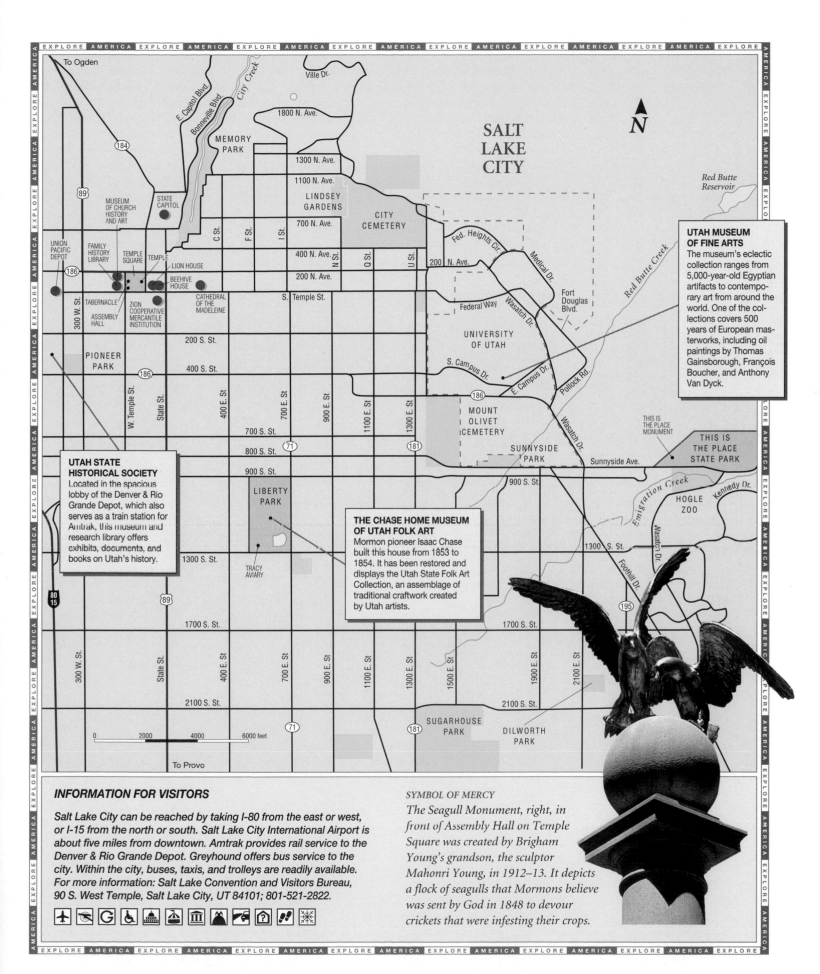

SALT LAKE CITY

To Ogden
Ville Dr.
City Creek
E. Capitol Blvd.
Bonneville Blvd.
1800 N. Ave.
MEMORY PARK
1300 N. Ave.
1100 N. Ave.
LINDSEY GARDENS
700 N. Ave.
CITY CEMETERY
MUSEUM OF CHURCH HISTORY AND ART
STATE CAPITOL
C St.
F St.
I St.
400 N. Ave.
N St.
Q St.
U St.
200 N. Ave.
Fed. Heights Cir.
Medical Dr.
Red Butte Reservoir
Red Butte Creek

UTAH MUSEUM OF FINE ARTS
The museum's eclectic collection ranges from 5,000-year-old Egyptian artifacts to contemporary art from around the world. One of the collections covers 500 years of European masterworks, including oil paintings by Thomas Gainsborough, François Boucher, and Anthony Van Dyck.

UNION PACIFIC DEPOT
FAMILY HISTORY LIBRARY
TEMPLE SQUARE
TEMPLE
LION HOUSE
BEEHIVE HOUSE
TABERNACLE
ASSEMBLY HALL
ZION COOPERATIVE MERCANTILE INSTITUTION
CATHEDRAL OF THE MADELEINE
S. Temple St.
Federal Way
Wasatch Dr.
Fort Douglas Blvd.
UNIVERSITY OF UTAH
300 W. St.
200 S. St.
PIONEER PARK
400 S. St.
W. Temple St.
State St.
400 E. St.
700 E. St.
900 E. St.
1100 E. St.
1300 E. St.
S. Campus Dr.
E. Campus Dr.
Pollock Rd.
700 S. St.
MOUNT OLIVET CEMETERY
Wasatch Dr.
THIS IS THE PLACE MONUMENT
THIS IS THE PLACE STATE PARK

UTAH STATE HISTORICAL SOCIETY
Located in the spacious lobby of the Denver & Rio Grande Depot, which also serves as a train station for Amtrak, this museum and research library offers exhibits, documents, and books on Utah's history.

800 S. St.
900 S. St.
LIBERTY PARK
SUNNYSIDE PARK
Sunnyside Ave.
900 S. St.
Emigration Creek
HOGLE ZOO
Kennedy Dr.

THE CHASE HOME MUSEUM OF UTAH FOLK ART
Mormon pioneer Isaac Chase built this house from 1853 to 1854. It has been restored and displays the Utah State Folk Art Collection, an assemblage of traditional craftwork created by Utah artists.

1300 S. St.
TRACY AVIARY
1300 S. St.
Foothill Dr.
Wasatch Dr.
1700 S. St.
1700 S. St.
2100 S. St.
2100 S. St.
300 W. St.
State St.
400 E. St.
700 E. St.
900 E. St.
1100 E. St.
1300 E. St.
1500 E. St.
1900 E. St.
2100 E. St.
SUGARHOUSE PARK
DILWORTH PARK
0 2000 4000 6000 feet
To Provo

INFORMATION FOR VISITORS

Salt Lake City can be reached by taking I-80 from the east or west, or I-15 from the north or south. Salt Lake City International Airport is about five miles from downtown. Amtrak provides rail service to the Denver & Rio Grande Depot. Greyhound offers bus service to the city. Within the city, buses, taxis, and trolleys are readily available. For more information: Salt Lake Convention and Visitors Bureau, 90 S. West Temple, Salt Lake City, UT 84101; 801-521-2822.

SYMBOL OF MERCY
The Seagull Monument, right, in front of Assembly Hall on Temple Square was created by Brigham Young's grandson, the sculptor Mahonri Young, in 1912–13. It depicts a flock of seagulls that Mormons believe was sent by God in 1848 to devour crickets that were infesting their crops.

SALT LAKE CITY 77

SIMPLE ABODE
The Fairbanks Home, above, was built in the 1850's for John B. Fairbanks, a prominent businessman and Mormon bishop. The house was restored and moved to This Is the Place State Park in the 1980's.

FLATTERING IMITATION
The four murals decorating the spandrels of the state capitol's 286-foot dome, right, depict pivotal figures in Utah history, including explorer John C. Frémont and Brigham Young. Richard K. A. Kletting, Utah's preeminent architect, based his design for the capitol on the U.S. Capitol in Washington, D.C. The building, located on a bluff above Temple Square, was dedicated in 1916.

ner of Temple Square outward. For example, 600 South 800 East is six blocks south and eight blocks east of the marker. Visitors quickly discover how well the system works as they navigate their way through this walkable city, especially once they realize they have only to glance up at the mountains to know which way is east.

As the city expanded, residents learned the fine art of balancing the intimate feel of a small town with the requirements of a metropolis. In recent years Salt Lake City has become one of the fastest-growing cities in America. Its inhabitants number about 172,000—the population of Salt Lake County has increased to almost 800,000—and it includes a great diversity of ethnic and religious groups. The city's wide streets, which were designed to permit a wagon team to turn around, seem less spacious than they once did. Although the Mormons have recruited converts from every part of the globe and some 9.7 million people call themselves Latter-day Saints, they now number slightly less than 50 percent of the city's population.

Today Salt Lake City offers a wide range of restaurants, theaters, and stores, as well as a major university. It enjoys a low crime rate, a booming economy, and a huge outdoor recreation area close enough to serve as a city park. When the weather gets hot, visitors can take refuge in alpine canyons,

such as Mill Creek, Little Cottonwood, and Big Cottonwood, within a cool zone of wildflower meadows and soaring rocks sliced by tumbling water. Salt Lake City bills itself as a mountain resort, and the nearby slopes of Alta, Snowbird, Solitude, and Brighton attract skiers in the winter.

In one of the oddest developments in its history, the greater Salt Lake area has become a suburb of Los Angeles, with some residents making the weekly 688-mile commute by air from their homes in Salt Lake to high-powered jobs in California.

CITY OF SAINTS

Salt Lake City still remains a Mormon enclave, and visitors who wish to learn about the city's roots should visit downtown's Temple Square, a complex that includes the Temple, the Tabernacle, the Assembly Hall, two visitor centers, and several large gardens set on 10 acres of prime real estate. At the nearby Museum of Church History and Art, visitors can learn about LDS history through interactive media, films, and puppet shows. Other church buildings stand in the immediate neighborhood—among them the

Family History Library, which is the world's most complete genealogical research facility. Although Temple Square is a mecca for Mormons, visitors are always welcome. This is because the LDS Church is, after all, a missionary church.

The Temple is built of gray granite and decorated with spires, crenellations, and round windows. It was completed in 1893 after 40 years of labor. Although the building resembles a cathedral, it is not used for worship; instead, it is divided into meeting rooms and other spaces that serve a variety of functions, including weddings for the living and baptisms for the dead. Only Mormons in good standing may enter the Temple itself.

The Tabernacle is open to all. Best known as the home of the Mormon Tabernacle Choir, it was built before the Temple, in 1867. The Tabernacle was constructed with limited local materials. Its domed roof, resembling an eggshell split lengthwise, is supported by wooden timbers that were steamed and then bent into their present shape. The gold-painted pipes of its great organ were constructed of wood, and the columns that support the circular balcony were painted to resemble

MONUMENTAL REFLECTION
The glass exterior of the new Zion Cooperative Mercantile Institution (ZCMI), above, reflects the contours of the LDS Office Building. On the left stands one of Brigham Young's homes, the Lion House; on the right, the pillars of the LDS Administration Building. ZCMI was set up by the church in 1868 "to bring goods here and sell them as low as they possibly can be sold," according to Young. The building has since been rebuilt as a modern shopping center.

CREEK OF LIFE

The Salt Lake City skyline, right, is set amid greenery and mountains. An irrigation system was the key to developing this city on the edge of the desert. In 1849 Capt. Howard Stansbury surveyed the area for the U.S. government. He wrote: "Through the city flows an unfailing stream of pure, sweet water, which by an ingenious mode of irrigation, is made to traverse each side of every street, spreading life, verdure and beauty."

marble. The acoustics are excellent: a pin dropped by the podium can be heard throughout the hall.

A similarly creative use of native materials can be seen at the Beehive House, from 1854 to 1877 Brigham Young's official residence, where he presided as territorial governor and then as president of the church. The house was not large enough to accommodate his entire family, which has been estimated to number about 27 wives and 57 children; some of them lived next door at Lion House. Although the walls of Beehive House are adobe, its structure reflects the style of Young's native New England, including even a widow's walk. All of the furnishings in the original building were either hand-crafted on-site or hauled across the plains by wagon. Brigham Young built his family dining room table from the bed of a Conestoga wagon.

MORMONS AND GENTILES

Some of the communities of non-Mormons (or Gentiles, as the Mormons refer to them) that make up Salt Lake City today are situated across the valley floor, south of Temple Square. This lively section of the city is peppered with restaurants that serve Mexican, Vietnamese, Chinese, Middle Eastern, and Indian cuisines. Scattered among the ethnic eateries are grocery stores selling *chicherones*, falafel, rice noodles, lemongrass, Indonesian curry sauce, and other exotic offerings.

GLORIOUS LIGHT

The stained-glass windows of the Cathedral of the Madeleine were created in 1906 by Zettler Studios of Munich, Germany. The church itself was built under Lawrence Scanlan, the first Catholic bishop of Utah. Salt Lake City is now home to about 60,000 Roman Catholics, many of whom are descendants of those who began coming here from Ireland in the 1890's.

Salt Lake City hosts a wide range of special events throughout the year. Among them are the Utah Winter Games in January, the Mexican-American community's Cinco de Mayo celebrations in May, and the Utah Arts Festival in June, which features concerts, dance performances, and a parade, below. The festival is celebrated next door to the French Renaissance–style Union Pacific Depot, built in 1909.

LIBERTY PARK

Liberty Park lies southeast of Temple Square and is bordered by 900 and 1300 South and 500 and 700 East. Its verdant grounds offer a getaway place for city dwellers on sweltering summer afternoons. Families picnic under the trees, footballs and Frisbees fly across the lawn, and the beat of drums played by young musicians fills the air. The pathways are crowded with joggers, inline skaters, and the occasional police officer on a mountain bike. Elderly Chinese move slowly through tai chi positions on the grass beneath the shady canopy of trees. In the park's southwestern corner, the Tracy Aviary rings with the braying and bellowing of its trademark hornbills. The aviary's feathered residents include flamingos, bald eagles, and golden pheasants from China. Some children toss bread to ducks and swans; others wander through the Lory Exhibit, where a flurry of hyacinthine macaws snatch fruit from outstretched hands. Youngsters can splash and wade in nearby Seven Canyons Fountain.

Children from all over the city participate in Salt Lake City's largest public celebration, the Days of '47, commemorating the July 24, 1847, arrival of the first pioneers. For all their visionary zeal, those

early pioneers could hardly have foreseen how their independent kingdom, wedged between the desert and the mountains, would metamorphose from a religious refuge into a great American city, a place where people of all walks of life could live in peace.

OTHER SITES & ATTRACTIONS

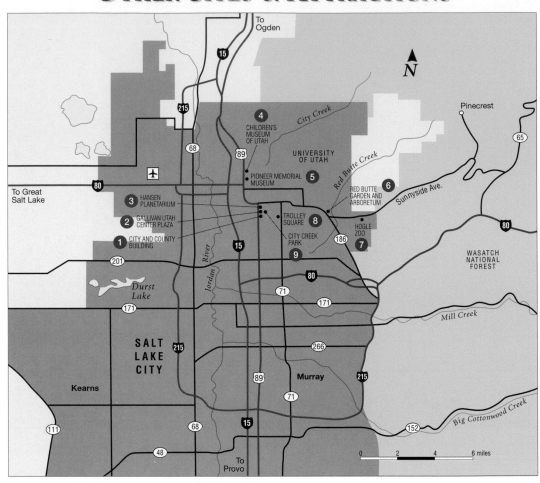

The Wasatch Range provides a dramatic backdrop for the turreted City and County Building and its clock tower, below.

1 CITY AND COUNTY BUILDING

Built in the 1890's, this structure is one of Salt Lake City's architectural treasures. From 1896 to 1916 it served as the state capitol, and it now houses city government offices. During the 1989 restoration, the structure was set on earthquake-resistant shock absorbers. The exterior is decorated with stone carvings of farmers and miners—important symbols of Utah history. The lavish interior contains more than 100 rooms. Located at 451 South State St.

2 GALLIVAN UTAH CENTER PLAZA

The Utah Center is billed as Salt Lake City's Outdoor Living Room. The center is a combination sculpture garden and plaza that includes an amphitheater, a pond used as a skating rink in the winter, an aviary, fountains, lawns, and a giant chessboard. The plaza also serves as a venue for festivals and performances. Located at 36 East St. at 200 South St.

3 HANSEN PLANETARIUM

For visitors with a penchant for stargazing, this planetarium offers a variety of astronomy programs, along with multimedia laser shows. The planetarium displays a six-foot-diameter globe of the earth and a Foucault pendulum that tracks the earth's rotation. Also on display are models of space shuttles and rockets, and a moon rock. An outreach program offers instruction in the use of telescopes. Located at 15 South State St.

4 CHILDREN'S MUSEUM OF UTAH

This museum's interactive exhibits explore aspects of science, art, and international culture. Children can shop in the miniature grocery store or pilot a passenger jet. A room devoted to the study of light features a phosphorescent-lit wall; when visitors stand against it, a strobe light produces a ghostlike image of their bodies. Other popular exhibits include a human-size hamster wheel, a giant piano that is played by walking on the keys, and antigravity mirrors. Located at 840 North 300 W.

5 PIONEER MEMORIAL MUSEUM

Built in 1950, this replica of the Salt Lake Theatre of the 1860's contains a variety of historic items, including dolls, handicrafts, military uniforms, rifles, clocks, toys, quilts, clothing, paintings, and tools. The Carriage House displays antique wagons, handcarts, a mule-drawn trolley, and farm equipment. Located at 300 North Main St.

6 RED BUTTE GARDEN AND ARBORETUM

Perched on the foothills of the Wasatch Range, this garden is divided into sections that display native and exotic plants. Banks of flowers line the Floral Walk. The herb, medicinal, and fragrance gardens feature plants used in cooking and healing. Visitors can stroll through a grove of conifer trees and explore a waterfall garden. An array of aquatic

plants thrives alongside the creek that bisects the park. Walking trails lead to 400 acres of land that have been maintained in their natural state. Located at 300 Wakara Way.

7 HOGLE ZOO

With more than 1,300 animals, the Hogle Zoo is one of the largest and most outstanding animal parks in the state. Among the zoo's most popular attractions are the World of Flight Bird Show and the Giant Animal Complex. Children can stroke the animals at the petting zoo. Located at 2600 Sunnyside Ave.

8 TROLLEY SQUARE

The rambling redbrick garages of Salt Lake's electric trolley system were built in 1908 and remained in use until 1945, when the trolleys stopped running. One of the structures was restored and remodeled in 1972; today it houses exhibits and artifacts that recall a time when trolleys were the primary means of transportation. Two restored trolley cars are displayed on a section of the original trolley tracks; another 1919 trolley car is housed within a restaurant. Another collection focuses on architectural items salvaged from Salt Lake City mansions; these include doors, staircases, a fireplace, etched glass windows, and a gazebo. Located at 700 East St.

9 CITY CREEK PARK

City Creek once flowed through Brigham Young's backyard, and its waters were used to nourish some of the first potato fields planted by pioneers. City Creek Park, together with Brigham Young Memorial Park across the street, provides a seminatural oasis of ponds and waterfalls in the middle of the steel and concrete of the downtown core. Historic exhibits feature a waterwheel and irrigation projects. Located at the junction of State St. and Second Ave.

City Creek, above, winds its way through downtown Salt Lake City, providing working men and women with a tranquil place to take a break.

Asteroid Landed Softly, left, is one of the many whimsical artworks on display in Gallivan Utah Center Plaza.

LOS ANGELES

With its vibrant mix of people from many different cultures, the City of Angels perpetually re-creates itself.

From the Griffith Observatory at night, the city of Los Angeles spreads out along glittering avenues of light that run as far as the eye can see. Some people say that each tiny light—flickering like a far-off star—represents the single dream of a resident of this city, the center of the show business galaxy. Ever since its sunny climes and idyllic setting on the edge of the Pacific attracted the first moviemaking crews in the early 1900's, Los Angeles has been a magnet for would-be entertainers and enthusiastic stargazers from around the globe.

Multitudes of worlds converge in L.A. On any given street corner, a person might hear Urdu, Ethiopian, German, or one of a hundred other languages being spoken. Forty percent of Los Angeles' population is foreign-born, making it more ethnically diverse, perhaps, than any city since ancient Rome. Yet Los Angeles remains a uniquely American place. It is a city of West Coast cool and restless innovation, of headline grabbers and trendsetters. But for outsiders and residents alike, this land of freeways, power lunches, movie stars, and palm trees is a city of dreams.

SHOP UNTIL THEY DROP
Cobblestone streets and European-style storefronts add flair to Beverly Hills' 2 Rodeo. This pedestrian street is an offshoot of Rodeo Drive, the world-famous street featured in Julia Roberts' shopping spree in the film Pretty Woman. *Rodeo Drive boasts such upscale shops and boutiques as Cartier, Tiffany, Valentino, Louis Vuitton, Christian Dior, and Giorgio Armani.*

TOWERS OF STEEL AND GLASS
Overleaf: The IBM and Wells Fargo office buildings are set amid the jumble of skyscrapers in Los Angeles' downtown. A leader in international trade, advertising, and computer programming, and the center of the entertainment industry, L.A. is also home to 176 colleges and universities.

"Some of these buildings are over 20 years old!" deadpans Steve Martin in the hit movie *L.A. Story* as he drives past palatial Beverly Hills homes. It's an observation that rings true. Los Angeles is not about yesterday—it's about today and tomorrow. Despite the tendency of Angelinos to demolish the past in order to build for the future, important parts of the city's rich history are still in plain view.

Olvera Street was once the mercantile district of the original settlement, a Spanish outpost founded in 1781 and most likely named El Pueblo de la Reina de Los Angeles, or Village of the Queen of the Angels. Today it is the core of El Pueblo de Los Angeles Historic Monument, located across from the Civic Center. Walking across stones that mark Zanja Madre, the fledgling town's first irrigation canal, visitors often are serenaded by Mexican bands. Travelers stroll past craft shops and vending wagons purveying Hispanic weavings, pottery, and utensils. The two dozen or so historic buildings in the area include a reconstruction of the 1818 Avila Adobe, Los Angeles' oldest house, and Old Plaza Church, the city's oldest church, built in 1822.

| ETHNIC VITALITY | Even from the outset, Los Angeles was culturally diverse: the city's founders, 44 Spanish, mulatto, black, and Indian set- |

tlers, were sent here by Felipe de Neve, New Spain's governor of California. By the end of the century, the coastal plain had been divided into land grants and quickly became a network of *ranchos*. The city itself grew slowly on an economy that traded in olives, dates, and tanned hides.

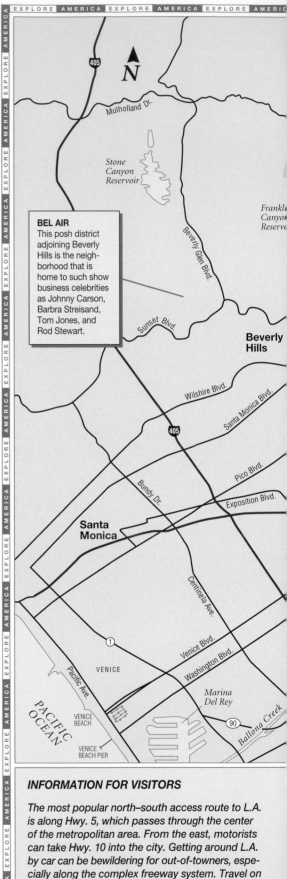

BEL AIR
This posh district adjoining Beverly Hills is the neighborhood that is home to such show business celebrities as Johnny Carson, Barbra Streisand, Tom Jones, and Rod Stewart.

INFORMATION FOR VISITORS

The most popular north–south access route to L.A. is along Hwy. 5, which passes through the center of the metropolitan area. From the east, motorists can take Hwy. 10 into the city. Getting around L.A. by car can be bewildering for out-of-towners, especially along the complex freeway system. Travel on the major boulevards is generally less confusing

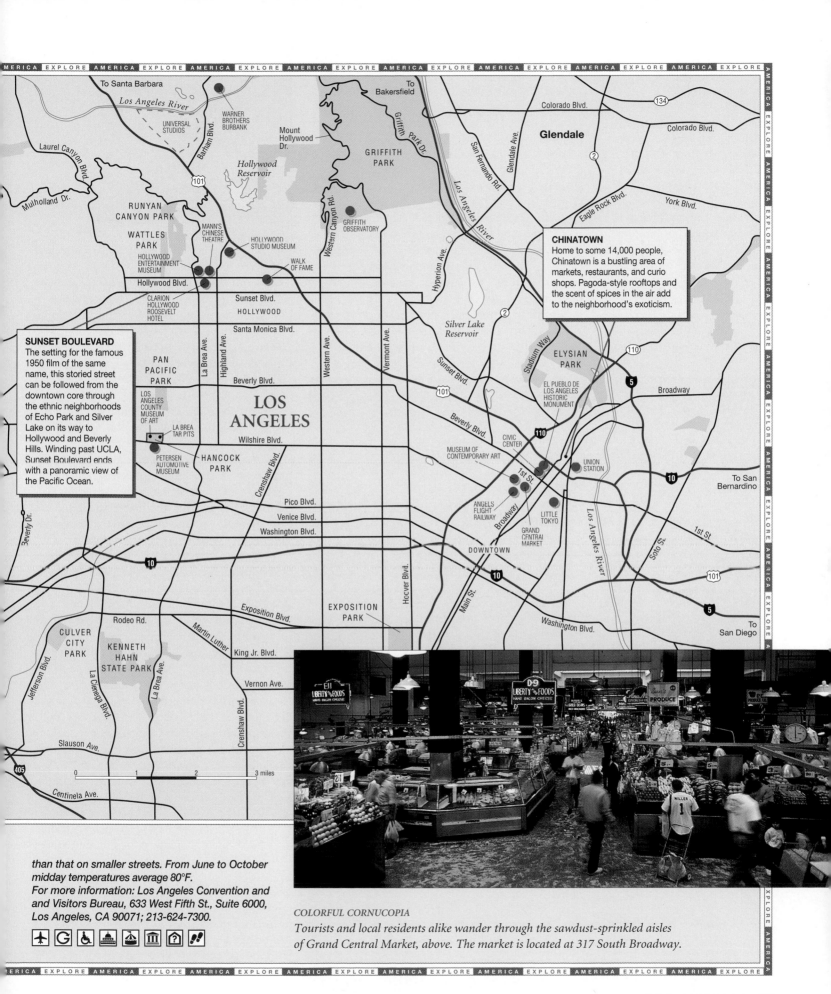

CHINATOWN
Home to some 14,000 people, Chinatown is a bustling area of markets, restaurants, and curio shops. Pagoda-style rooftops and the scent of spices in the air add to the neighborhood's exoticism.

SUNSET BOULEVARD
The setting for the famous 1950 film of the same name, this storied street can be followed from the downtown core through the ethnic neighborhoods of Echo Park and Silver Lake on its way to Hollywood and Beverly Hills. Winding past UCLA, Sunset Boulevard ends with a panoramic view of the Pacific Ocean.

than that on smaller streets. From June to October midday temperatures average 80°F.
For more information: Los Angeles Convention and and Visitors Bureau, 633 West Fifth St., Suite 6000, Los Angeles, CA 90071; 213-624-7300.

COLORFUL CORNUCOPIA
Tourists and local residents alike wander through the sawdust-sprinkled aisles of Grand Central Market, above. The market is located at 317 South Broadway.

ERICA EXPLORE AMERICA EXPLORE AMERICA EXPLORE AMERICA EXPLORE AMERICA EXPLORE AMERICA EXPLORE AMERICA EXPLORE AMERICA EXPLORE AMERICA EXPLORE AMERICA EXPLORE AMERICA EXPLORE

LOS ANGELES 87

California was granted statehood in 1850 and, with the subsequent arrival of the railroads, settlers began to pour in. Sporadic land booms, beginning in the 1880's, brought tens of thousands of Americans who were eager to take advantage of the cheap real estate and the region's pleasant climate. New towns sprang up from the arid floodplains and, as the towns grew in size, they gradually formed the nation's largest contiguous urban area.

Los Angeles sits at the center of the Los Angeles Five–County area, which stretches some 34,149 square miles. With more than 14 million people living there, the Five-County area is more populated than all but three states. The nation's second-largest city, Los Angeles recently surpassed New York as the primary port of entry for immigrants,

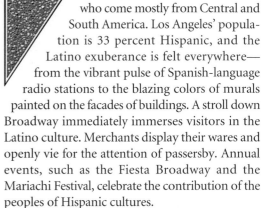

who come mostly from Central and South America. Los Angeles' population is 33 percent Hispanic, and the Latino exuberance is felt everywhere—from the vibrant pulse of Spanish-language radio stations to the blazing colors of murals painted on the facades of buildings. A stroll down Broadway immediately immerses visitors in the Latino culture. Merchants display their wares and openly vie for the attention of passersby. Annual events, such as the Fiesta Broadway and the Mariachi Festival, celebrate the contribution of the peoples of Hispanic cultures.

But Latinos are not alone in finding new opportunities in Los Angeles. A visit to the lively Grand Central Market, with its dozens of stalls selling ethnic foods, is like taking a culinary trip around the world. Los Angeles has the largest Japanese population outside Japan. Little Tokyo, located east of the market along San Pedro Street, is a low-key mix of residential homes, businesses, and affordable sushi bars. At the Japanese American Cultural and Community Center, exhibitions, and dance and theater performances regularly take place amid the rock sculptures and sunken gardens. The nearby California Plaza, a modern complex designed by Japanese architect Arata Isozaki, is home to the Museum of Contemporary Art. The museum complex contains an extraordinary sampling of works from abstract Expressionist, Pop, and other modern art movements. By balancing the spare esthetics of traditional Japanese artistic sensibilities with Los Angeles' homegrown love for the outlandish, this museum represents the perfect expression of the city's multicultural makeup.

LIGHTS, CAMERA, ACTION!

When Kansas prohibitionist Horace Wilcox plotted a town site at Cahuenga Pass in 1887, he envisioned a community based on sobriety and high moral standards. Wilcox named his burgeoning town Hollywood, and within the space of a generation the town had become synonymous with glamour and excess. Hollywood's transformation from humble farmland to a field of dreams is

simple—it was tailor-made for the film industry. The weather was mild, the landscape was diverse, and the proximity to Mexico offered film producers a fast means of escape from the likes of East Coast attorneys, who attempted to enforce Thomas Edison's patent on the use of the movie camera.

In 1913 pioneers D. W. Griffith and Cecil B. DeMille went to Hollywood to shoot films for nickelodeons—small movie houses that showed Wild West train robberies and damsels-in-distress for five cents a movie. These early filmmakers shocked Hollywood's staid residents with their bohemian lifestyle, flamboyant dress, and incessant pranks: local lore has it that director Mack Sennett and his Keystone Kops frequently dumped oil at intersections to create spontaneous accidents, thus creating the first slapstick comedies. Despite local ordinances against rowdy behavior, the moviemakers stayed on and, within a few short years, the flimsy sets that had been set up in barns and empty lots became full-fledged film factories. Soon the attention of the entire world was focused on glamorous cinematic stars as they alighted from their elegant limousines to attend grand film openings at the theaters along Hollywood Boulevard.

Movie buffs especially enjoy walking along the fabled Walk of Fame, the promenade at Hollywood and Vine that recognizes actors, actresses, producers, directors, and others associated with the

CITY OF ANGELS
Los Angeles at night is a sea of twinkling lights, above, reaching to the distant horizon. With a population of more than 3.5 million, Los Angeles boasts the largest concentration of people of all the 80 incorporated cities within the Los Angeles Five–County area. Vernon, the smallest community, has fewer than 80 residents.

TUMBLING WATERS
The stepped pyramid fountain, left, outside the Museum of Contemporary Art complements the pyramids and cubes of the building. In 1991 the American Institute of Architects named the building 1 of the 10 best works of American architecture constructed since 1980.

film business. Each is honored with a star that bears his or her name. The Hollywood Entertainment Museum features film clips and curios from the golden age of motion pictures, along with the studio sets from such successful television series as *Star Trek* and *Cheers*. The Hollywood Studio Museum houses the barn where Hollywood's first feature-length film, DeMille's *The Squaw Man* was shot in 1913. The Clarion Hollywood Roosevelt Hotel displays historic photos in its lobby, where screen legends such as Charlie Chaplin and Douglas Fairbanks once trod, while the plaza in front of Grauman's (now Mann's) Chinese Theatre boasts the handprints and footprints of movie stars.

In the early days, visitors to Universal Studios could watch directors shoot scenes for their silent films. Now the studio is an entertainment complex and amusement park offering rides and attractions based on movie plots—visitors can participate in re-creations of scenes from *Jurassic Park* and *Back to the Future*. At the nearby Warner Brothers Burbank studio, fans can tour sets, visit a museum of memorabilia from Warner films such as *Casablanca,* and watch a production in progress.

For many visitors, however, the highlight of a trip to Hollywood is cruising the palm-lined residential avenues of neighboring Beverly Hills with a Star Map bought from a street vendor, on the off chance of glimpsing an Oscar winner inspecting the garden or collecting the morning paper. Enterprising tour operators have designed circuits that cater to all tastes, from the reverent to the macabre. One group visits the graves of Rudolph Valentino and Marilyn Monroe—in a hearse.

Of course, Los Angeles isn't solely about making movies—it is also a center of television, music,

LATIN RHYTHMS
Historic Olvera Street, left, a bustling pedestrian alley, resembles a Mexican marketplace. Located in the heart of El Pueblo de Los Angeles Historic Monument, the street is frequently the site of fiestas.

and live comedy. Television fans can watch tapings of popular shows, including *Seinfeld*, or drive by television landmarks, including the home featured in *The Brady Bunch* series and the high school made famous in *Beverly Hills 90210*. Nighttime offerings range from sidesplitting stand-up routines at comedy clubs still frequented by the likes of Jay Leno and Roseanne to musical shows at the House of Blues and the Hollywood Bowl.

MIRACLE MILE

Detroit may have built the car, but the car built Los Angeles. By the 1940's the region had assumed a suburban sprawl that only intensified with the construction of freeways—the city's most familiar emblem. A drive down Wilshire Boulevard traces this remarkable story. The road was first an ancient Indian trail, then a path that served as a route for Spanish padres heading toward the coast. As the path evolved, it became a road that linked the expanding city to the sea. In the 1920's Wilshire's Miracle Mile became the nation's first commercial district to grow up along a major thoroughfare. The district featured the first suburban department stores, parking lots, and synchronized stoplights. Soon elegant hotels and country clubs lined the street. The grand

PIER ON THE PACIFIC
Venice Beach Pier, left, is silhouetted by a pink sky at sunset. In the daytime the Venice Beach boardwalk takes on a carnival atmosphere that attracts thousands of strollers, cyclists, and inline skaters. The 22-mile Beach Bikeway stretches from Santa Monica down the coast to Redondo Beach.

homes of Larchmont and Fremont Circle, and such renovated Art Deco architectural masterpieces as the Wiltern Theater, attest to the area's heyday.

One of the highlights of the Miracle Mile is Museum Row. The George C. Page Museum of La Brea Discoveries, located in Hancock Park, preserves an unusual slice of ancient history. During the Pleistocene epoch, some 40,000 years ago, this area was a swampy savannah filled with crude-oil seeps and shallow asphalt pits. The intense summer heat caused the asphalt to melt into a sticky goo, trapping unwary animals like horses and antelopes. Saber-toothed cats and other predators in search of an easy meal were pulled under with their prey, as were the scavengers that followed. None escaped. Winter flooding covered the death trap with sediment before the hot weather returned and renewed the cycle. So far, excavations at the La Brea Tar Pits have unearthed more than 1.5 million vertebrate and 2.5 million invertebrate fossils representing 150 species of plants and more than 500 species of animals, including mammoths and giant ground sloths. Visitors can view many of these creatures by descending into the museum's eerie subterranean bunker. During the summer excavation season, the museum allows observers to watch paleontologists at work in Pit 91.

The adjacent Los Angeles County Museum of Art preserves history—in oils of a different sort. Founded in 1910 and enhanced by major bequests, the County Museum is the largest museum west of Chicago. The heart of the huge complex is the Ahmanson Building, whose four-story atrium opens onto galleries containing everything from ancient Chinese ceramics and Assyrian reliefs to engravings by Albrecht Dürer. The newer buildings in the complex display a grouping of renowned photographs and the museum's growing collection of works by 20th-century artists, including

CITY WITHIN A CITY
Brilliant purple blossoms cloak a jacaranda tree, above, in residential Beverly Hills. An independent city surrounded by Los Angeles, Beverly Hills was once home to movie stars Mary Pickford and Douglas Fairbanks Sr.

SHORTLINE RAILROAD
The Angels Flight Railway, in the heart of downtown L.A., charges 25 cents for the world's shortest ride on a rail line. The railway takes visitors from Pershing Subway Station up Bunker Hill to the Water Court at California Plaza.

Pablo Picasso, Robert Rauschenberg, and Andy Warhol. The Pavilion for Japanese Art boasts the most important collection of Edo period screen and scroll paintings outside Japan, a reminder of the important contributions of the Pacific Rim cultures in the shaping of the city and region.

The Petersen Automotive Museum, located across the street from the pavilion, explores the role that the car has played in the history of Los Angeles. More than 200 vintage cars, trucks, and motorcycles are on display. Visitors can walk alongside life-size re-creations of service stations, car showrooms, and custom body shops from L.A.'s past. These full-scale street scenes illustrate the impact that cars have had on culture, urban planning, home life, youth, and the dining habits of Americans. A design studio offers a look at the futuristic prototypes of the vehicles of tomorrow.

The automobile may occupy a central place in the California psyche, but at least one Angelino staked his future in gondolas. In 1904 entrepreneur Abbot Kinney hit upon the idea of building an amusement park and vacation city on a series of canals, and the Venice of America was born. Like the Italian original, Kinney's town featured graceful bridges, hotels and dance halls, elegant arcades, and opulent canalside vacation bungalows. As a publicity stunt, Kinney imported Italian gondoliers. Unfortunately, nearby oil drilling and stagnant water troubles led to Venice's demise in the 1920's. The theme park closed, many of the canals were filled in, and for years the town itself drifted in a state of semi-abandonment.

Today Venice's offbeat charm makes it one of L.A.'s hotter neighborhoods, attracting everyone from artists and actors to beach bums and bodybuilders. Six of the canals have been refurbished and are now lined with high-priced homes. Main Street's trendy boutiques and delightful eateries beckon visitors to bask in laid-back contentment. People from every part of the globe enjoy strolling along the popular Ocean Front Walk, commonly known as the boardwalk, where cafés and shops form the backdrop for an endless procession of local eccentrics, from turbaned inline skaters playing electric guitars to blindfolded chain saw jugglers. Bodybuilders pump iron in outdoor weight rooms and athletes play pickup basketball games for scores of onlookers.

| STARRY EYES, BIG DREAMS | A slow drive at sunset along Mulholland Drive winds high above the sprawling city, offering tantalizing glimpses of the |

mansions perched precariously on the hillsides. The grand boulevards below seem to pour toward the sea in a flood of lights, and the San Fernando

Valley laps up against the snow-frosted San Gabriel Mountains. From on high, the first stars are seen struggling to penetrate the urban glow, while far below, a million dreams collide, intersect, and merge to create a sparkling new galaxy.

MODERN CITYSCAPE
The fluid forms of a modern sculpture, above, play off the boxy shapes of tall skyscrapers in the city's downtown area. The sculpture, titled Ulysses, *was created by Alexander Liberman in 1980.*

HAPPY NEW YEAR
A pair of gaily dressed celebrants, left, in the annual Golden Dragon Parade help ring in the Chinese New Year. The lively parade is held in Los Angeles' Chinatown in mid-February.

OTHER SITES & ATTRACTIONS

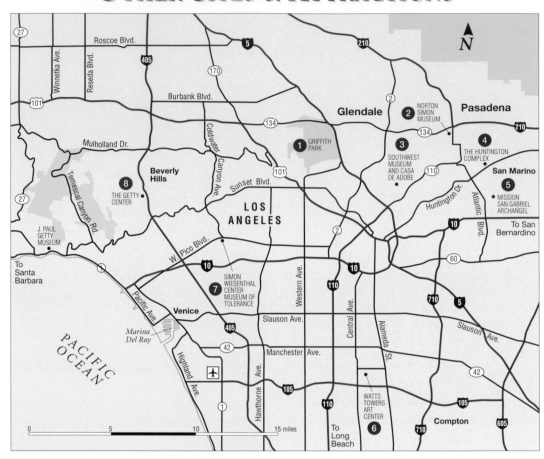

The J. Paul Getty Museum, below, replicates the Villa dei Papyri at Herculaneum in Italy. The original villa had been buried under ash following the eruption of Mount Vesuvius in A.D. 79. The museum's building and grounds are undergoing renovation and will reopen in 2001. During the restoration the collection will be on display at the Getty Center in Los Angeles.

1 GRIFFITH PARK

British entrepreneur Griffith Jenkins Griffith donated five square miles of mountain woodland to the people of Los Angeles in 1896 as "a resort for the rank and file." The nation's largest urban park is home to the Los Angeles Zoo, the Greek Theatre, the famed "Hollywood" sign, as well as the Griffith Observatory—an Art Deco landmark building that offers public viewings of stars, planetarium shows, and the best nighttime vistas of the city. Travel Town Museum, at the northern end of the park, preserves vintage trains from bygone eras. Located on I-5 at Los Feliz Blvd. in Los Angeles.

2 NORTON SIMON MUSEUM

Located in the heart of historic Pasadena, the Norton Simon Museum houses one of the world's premier collections of European masterpieces from the Renaissance to the 20th century, including paintings by Raphael, Botticelli, and El Greco. Impressionist and post-Impressionist works by Cezanne, Degas, Van Gogh, and Gauguin occupy a prominent place in the intimate galleries designed by Frank Gehry. Outstanding sculptures from South Asia, as well as works by Rodin, Brancusi, and Moore, are on exhibit inside the museum and in the sculpture garden. Located at 411 West Colorado Blvd. in Pasadena.

③ SOUTHWEST MUSEUM AND CASA DE ADOBE

The city of Los Angeles' oldest museum sits atop Mount Washington in Highland Park. Since 1914 archeologists have been contributing Native North American art and artifacts, as well as meso-American and South American pre-Columbian pottery and textiles, to this Mission Revival–style building. The nearby Casa de Adobe, built in 1918, re-creates the world of a 19th-century California *rancho* with period furnishings and craft demonstrations. Located at 234 Museum Dr. in Los Angeles.

④ THE HUNTINGTON COMPLEX

This famed cultural and educational center offers relief from the bustle of the metropolis. Created by railroad tycoon Henry Huntington and his wife, Arabella, the estate boasts more than 10 extraordinary botanical gardens; a world-renowned research library with rare manuscripts by Chaucer and Shakespeare; and a Beaux-Arts mansion, which houses a collection of American and British art that includes the famous *Pinkie* by Sir Thomas Lawrence and *The Blue Boy* by Thomas Gainsborough. One of the gardens contains more than 1,500 rose cultivars, many dating from medieval times. Located at 1151 Oxford Rd. in San Marino.

⑤ MISSION SAN GABRIEL ARCHANGEL

Established in 1771, Mission San Gabriel was one of Spain's four original outposts in Alta California. Today visitors can admire a restored Moorish-influenced church, a bell tower containing six bells dating back to the 18th century, and the only known paintings by local Indians in the mission system. The fortress-style mission features capped buttresses and long narrow windows. The well-preserved interior is painted in red, gold, and green. In September La Fiesta de San Gabriel celebrates the mission's founding with performances by folkloric dancers. Located at 537 West Mission Dr. in San Gabriel.

Visitors to the Griffith Observatory in Griffith Park, above, can gaze up at a re-creation of the night sky. A twin refracting telescope is made available to the public on clear evenings during the summer months.

⑥ WATTS TOWERS ART CENTER

Italian immigrant Simon Rodia built several fanciful towers over a period of 33 years. Rodia used junk items salvaged from the vicinity and affixed them to a mortared steel frame, creating an urban landmark of inspired whimsy and surreal beauty. Located at 1727 East 107th St. in Los Angeles.

⑦ SIMON WIESENTHAL CENTER MUSEUM OF TOLERANCE

The goal of this acclaimed educational center, opened in 1993, is to use technology and community outreach programs to promote tolerance, understanding, and human rights. The museum offers films and interactive displays on racial tolerance. It also contains dramatic art installations that focus on the Holocaust, providing an evocative illustration of the disastrous impact bigotry has on the human spirit. Located at 9786 West Pico Blvd. in Roxbury.

⑧ J. PAUL GETTY MUSEUM AT THE GETTY CENTER

"The Getty," perched above the city on its new billion-dollar campus, is one of the world's preeminent art institutions, offering a state-of-the-art facility for art history research, conservation, and public art education. The soaring atriums, skylighted galleries, and intimate pavilions house an extensive collection of paintings by European masters, including Titian, Rembrandt, Cezanne, and Van Gogh, as well as precious illuminated manuscripts of the Middle Ages and rare drawings by Michelangelo and Degas. The complex also displays treasures of furniture, sculpture, and photography. Located at 1200 Getty Center Dr. in Los Angeles.

The interior of the 19th-century Japanese House at The Huntington Complex, left, displays traditional Japanese furnishings. The house is situated within the Japanese Garden and overlooks a drum bridge that spans a koi pond.

SAN FRANCISCO

*This city of trolley cars and hilly
streets revels in the startling beauty
of its oceanside setting.*

Maybe it's the way the wind plays around
the city, singing in and out of its sun-
ribboned hills, then breathing wisps of sea fog
into unexpected corners, carrying the smell of
the ocean as a reminder of far-off places. Or
maybe it's the romantic cityscape, with its narrow, hilly streets and rows of Victorian houses,
its European cafés, and the flower shops that spill
their bouquets onto the sidewalks. Sometimes it
almost seems as if this peninsular enclave wedged
between San Francisco Bay and the vast Pacific—
wellspring of the Beat Generation, the Haight
Ashbury hippies, and now the New Agers—might
float off into never-never land. Whatever the
source of San Francisco's unique appeal, this
shimmering mirage of a city—*the* City, as its
fiercely loyal residents prefer to call it—has a compelling personality all its own.

No simple description fits a city as varied as
San Francisco, where each neighborhood, from
the working class Mission District to the gay and
free-spirited neighborhood known as the Castro,

PACIFIC OCEAN

Golden

CLIFF HOUSE
With its magnificent view of the Pacific Ocean and Ocean Beach, this popular restaurant is a magnet for visitors. The present neoclassical building was erected in 1909 by Emma Sutro on the site of the original 1881 Cliff House belonging to her father, Adolph Sutro, a self-made millionaire and onetime mayor of San Francisco. The building belongs to the National Park Service.

CHINA BEACH

PALACE OF THE LEGION OF HONOR · El Camino Del Mar

LINCOLN PARK · Legion of Honor Dr. · California St.

SEAL ROCKS

Geary St.

47th St. · 41st St. · 36th St. · 32nd St. · 28th St. · 24th St.

Balboa St.

Fulton St.

Spreckels Lake

John F. Kennedy Dr.

OCEAN BEACH

GOLDEN GATE PARK

Martin Luther King

Lincoln St.

Judah St.

Great Highway

Sunset Blvd.

Lawton St.

47th St. · 41st St. · 32nd St. · 28th St.

Noriega St.

RALLYING POINT
Union Square, above, acquired its name from a rally held here during the Civil War, when demonstrators pledged their loyalty to the Union. The granite shaft in the center of the square commemorates another conflict, honoring Adm. George Dewey's victory at Manila Bay in the Philippines during the Spanish-American War.

has its own heart, its own style, sometimes even its own weather and geography—and certainly its own history. The Spanish were the first Europeans to settle on the peninsula, claiming it in the 1770's for God and Empire. Close on their heels came the homesteaders, real estate entrepreneurs, "49ers" headed for the Sierra goldfields, Chinese immigrants fleeing starvation and the Opium Wars, and railroad barons. In its own way, each group has left its unmistakable mark on the city.

UNION SQUARE

One of San Francisco's benefactors was Gold Rush–era mayor John White Geary who, in 1850, donated 2.6 acres of sandy land to be used as a public square. Now called Union Square, this unusually level meeting place in such a hilly city is a perfect spot for visitors to get their bearings. Chic boutiques and galleries jostle

STREETS OF SAN FRANCISCO
Overleaf: Victorian houses line up along one of the streets crisscrossing the city's 47 hills. Between trips out to sea, fishing vessels are moored off Fisherman's Wharf, right.

NICKI T.

GOLDEN GA

SAN GIUSEPPE

VIRGIN

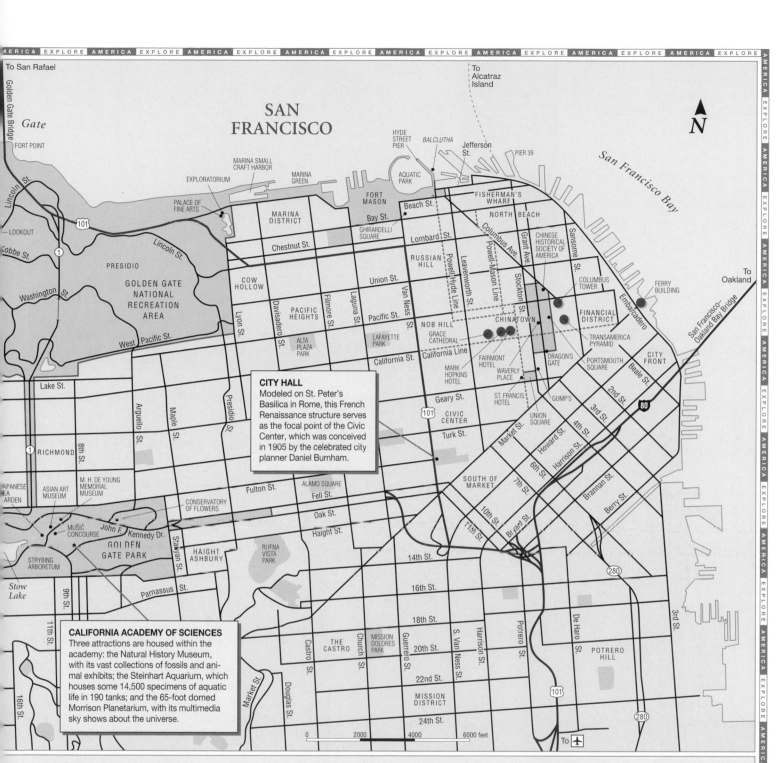

SAN FRANCISCO

CITY HALL
Modeled on St. Peter's Basilica in Rome, this French Renaissance structure serves as the focal point of the Civic Center, which was conceived in 1905 by the celebrated city planner Daniel Burnham.

CALIFORNIA ACADEMY OF SCIENCES
Three attractions are housed within the academy: the Natural History Museum, with its vast collections of fossils and animal exhibits; the Steinhart Aquarium, which houses some 14,500 specimens of aquatic life in 190 tanks; and the 65-foot domed Morrison Planetarium, with its multimedia sky shows about the universe.

INFORMATION FOR VISITORS

The main north–south route through California is I-5, which passes 50 miles east of San Francisco and is linked to the city via I-580. Hwy. 1 and Hwy. 101 also run north–south along the California coast. The main route from the east is I-80, which runs via Sacramento all the way from Chicago. County buses, airport shuttle minibuses, and taxis connect the city and San Francisco International Airport, which is about 15 miles away. All Greyhound services use the Transbay Terminal on Mission St. Amtrak trains stop across the bay in Richmond. The San Francisco Municipal Railway, or Muni, runs the city's public network of buses, trolley cars, cable cars, and underground trains, which become streetcars when they exit from the downtown metro system and head out to the suburbs. Visitors who drive around the city should turn their wheels into the curb when parking on a steep gradient. Drivers can circuit all the major city districts and neighborhoods as well as the waterfront area by taking the 49-mile Drive, which is marked by blue-and-white seagull signs. Maps of the route are available from the Visitor Information Center on Market St. at Powell.

For more information: San Francisco Convention and Visitors Bureau, 201 Third St., Suite 900, San Francisco, CA 94103-3185; 415-974-6900. San Francisco Visitor Information Center, 900 Market St., San Francisco, CA 94102; 415-391-2000.

ROMAN RUIN
The Palace of Fine Arts, right, was erected for the 1915 Panama Pacific Exposition. The classical-style rotunda survived until the 1960's, when decay demanded that it be replaced. Casts were made of the original and a duplicate was created in concrete. In 1969 a science and art museum, called the Exploratorium and founded by the renowned physicist Frank Oppenheimer, was built behind it.

BRIGHT LIGHTS
Chinatown's Grant Avenue, below, offers visitors a multitude of restaurants and souvenir shops.

for space among department stores and such turn-of-the-century institutions as the posh St. Francis Hotel and Gump's, named for founder Solomon Gump, who set up shop here in 1861. The store is now famous for antique and contemporary Asian treasures, master crafts of glass and ceramic, and its collections of pearls, jades, and corals.

CHINA-TOWN North of Union Square, the streets become narrower. At Grant Avenue, Dragon's Gate, donated to the community by the government of Taiwan and bedizened with dragons, arches over the street and welcomes visitors to the cacophony of Chinatown. More than 80,000 people live between this gateway and Columbus Avenue to the north. The neighborhood's rich tumble of sights, sounds, and smells goes on for blocks. Grocers hang roasted duck and pork in their shop windows. Outdoor produce stalls draw hordes of eager shoppers who pick through overflowing boxes of rosy-spiked litchis, bright purple aubergines, and snow peas, testing them for freshness. In side-street shops that specialize in traditional Chinese medicine, herbalists sort through their myriad drawers of dried plant and animal elixirs, carefully measuring out the ingredients and weighing them on scales.

Chinatown's enormous import emporiums are crammed from floor to ceiling with porcelain, jade, jewelry, and countless other items. In the neighborhood's many restaurants, chopstick-wielding diners of every nationality enjoy meals of succulent Peking duck, spicy Szechuan pork, and a particular favorite of the lunch crowd, dim sum. These snacks of steamed and fried dumplings, chicken feet, and other delectable offerings are served from trolleys wheeled to each table by white-jacketed waiters and waitresses.

Chinatown, like so much of the rest of San Francisco, was destroyed in the terrible fire that swept through the city as a result of the 1906 earthquake. Many of today's colorful and ornate facades date from the period of rapid rebuilding that followed the quake. On Waverly Place, west of Grant Avenue, lavishly painted balconies overhang the street. A dilapidated set of stairs leads up into the quiet serenity of the Jeng Sen, a Taoist and Buddhist temple whose walls, floor, and furniture are painted red to symbolize happiness and good fortune. Incense sweetens the air, curling around the golden statues of Buddha.

Chinese immigrants first came to San Francisco in the late 1840's to work in the goldfields. The next wave of Chinese arrived in the 1860's to build the transcontinental railroad. Their willingness to work for low wages gave rise to resentment and intensified racial bigotry. Oppressive legislation followed. In 1882 the U.S. Congress passed the Chinese Exclusion Acts, which banned new immigration from China—even the wives and children of the men already here. San Francisco's Chinatown became a bachelor society, inhabited by men parted from their families for life. The Exclusion Acts stayed on the books until 1943, and today, aged survivors of that ordeal can be seen hunched over chessboards in Portsmouth Square.

Chinatown is now the city's most affluent ethnic community; Asian-Americans bustle in and out of the skyscrapers that crowd the adjacent Financial District. Photographs and artifacts chronicling the history of the Chinese in the United States

WEATHER PATTERNS
Morning light illuminates the city's skyline viewed from San Francisco Bay, below. Surrounded on three sides by water, San Francisco has a remarkably stable climate: daytime temperatures rarely vary by more than a few degrees above or below 60°F. Heavy fogs are prevalent in the summer, while torrential rains occur in the winter.

are on display in the Chinese Historical Society of America, located at the northern end of Chinatown on Commercial Street.

West of Chinatown, the old-money neighborhood of sedate brownstones known as Nob Hill crouches precariously on its hilly perch. Anchoring the crest of the 338-foot hill is the French Gothic glory of Grace Cathedral, the third-largest Episcopal cathedral in the United States. Its 16-foot-tall doors are full-scale replicas of the Gates of Paradise made for Florence's Baptistry by Lorenzo Ghiberti. The doors open into an interior illuminated by light pouring through the stained-glass of the east rose window, which was made in Chartres, France.

FANCY HOTELS The city sparkles with refracted light when viewed from Top of the Mark, the splashy Art Deco bar located at the top of Nob Hill's Mark Hopkins Hotel, built in 1927. Just across the street stands the Italian Renaissance marble splendor of the Fairmont Hotel. Gutted in the 1906 fire, the Fairmont's interior was rebuilt by Julia Morgan, better known as the architect of William Randolph Hearst's lavish mansion in San Simeon, California.

It was Nob Hill's vertical cable car line that originally made the neighborhood on the summit inhabitable. Constructed in the 1870's to negotiate San Francisco's hills, the cable line helped make

AMERICAN PAGODA
Japanese landscape designer Makoto Hagiwara created the Japanese Tea Garden and its pagoda, above, in Golden Gate Park for the Japanese Village exhibit of the California Midwinter International Exposition of 1894.

STAR ATTRACTIONS
Sea lions at Pier 39, right, add to the carnival-like atmosphere of Fisherman's Wharf. The pier, which is the length of about three football fields, is now the site of two levels of restaurants and specialty shops.

sense of city plans that were conceived by the mid-19th-century city designer Jasper O'Farrell, who took no notice of the low Coast Range. Instead he gridded the hills with streets that march straight up and down the steep inclines.

From Nob Hill, the cable cars on the Powell-Mason Line swoop down dramatically toward the Golden Gate. Gripmen on this line tug and strain as they hand-operate the releases that hook each car to the cables that move below street level at a constant 9.5 miles an hour. As the cable cars make their way to the water, the line inches up and over Russian Hill, past the well-tended, gentrified row houses. In the 1890's Nob Hill's intellectual community included short-story writer Ambrose Bierce and Ina Coolbrith, California's first poet laureate. These days the neighborhood's main attraction is Lombard Street, which twists through eight switch-backs as it winds down the southwestern flank of Russian Hill. Visitors also flock to Macondry Lane, made famous as Barbary Lane in Armistead Maupin's *Tales of the City*, the wry soap opera of San Francisco life during the early 1970's.

FURTHER TALES OF THE CITY

On the north side of Russian Hill the landscape flattens out dramatically—and artificially. It was landfill that created the extended level expanses that now rim the city's north shore, where Fisherman's Wharf, a great tourist mecca, is located. Out in the bay the daunting face of "The Rock"—Alcatraz Island—cuts into the northern horizon, while to the east, the Bay Bridge sweeps in an 8.4-mile arc from the city to the hills of the East Bay. Along Hyde Street Pier, five historic ships (three of which are open to the public) are berthed, recalling San Francisco's maritime heyday. The most graceful among them is the stately, three-masted square-rigger *Balclutha*. Setting sail from Glasgow in 1886, it made 17 turns around Cape Horn carrying European hardware, coal, and wines to California and California-grown wheat back to Europe.

At the turn of the century the Ghirardelli brothers moved their chocolate factory into a large complex near the wharf. The irresistible smell of chocolate wafted through the air of the area for half a century until the early 1960's, when the business was moved to San Leandro. But the brothers' cavernous redbrick complex still anchors the west side of the wharf, its interior now filled with craft shops, specialty boutiques, and cafés where latte aficionados ruminate over their frothy brews.

Much of the north shore of the city is protected within the Golden Gate National Recreation Area (GGNRA), with its 74,000 acres scattered throughout bay lands. Many of its attractions, such as Fort

CLOISTERED WORLD
Garden greenery spills over the wrought-iron fence of a house, below, in Pacific Heights, one of the most exclusive neighborhoods in San Francisco.

TOWERS OF POWER
A cable car chugs up California Street, left, in San Francisco's Financial District. At the foot of the street lies the old Southern Pacific Building.

Mason, which sprawls beside Fisherman's Wharf, were originally military installations. Once the major embarkation facility for U.S. military personnel serving in the Pacific during World War II, Fort Mason's barracks and warehouses now are filled with the offices of arts organizations, small ethnic museums, and innovative theaters.

MARINA DISTRICT

Farther along this short but impressive stretch of coastline, the grassy expanses of Marina Green draw kite flyers, Frisbee throwers, and dog walkers. Just offshore, a sea breeze hums through the strait of the Golden Gate, propelling a flock of sailboats that tack back and forth beneath the Golden Gate Bridge. The wind sends in a billowing balloon of fog that obscures the bridge's orange evanescence and makes the distant foghorns bellow their sad, sweet song.

Behind Marina Green a warren of curving streets, edged by colored stucco houses, adds a touch of the Mediterranean to the neighborhood. Built on landfill that will turn to jelly in any major earthquake, these homes are a monument to the city's insouciant, live-for-today credo. Chestnut Street is the main commercial thoroughfare in the Marina District, with its delis selling imported cheeses and fresh pastas, its browser-friendly bookstores, and, of course, its countless cafés.

The hills just above the Marina are called Cow Hollow for the herds of cows and the tanneries that once were a common sight here. However, the area's bovine past has long since given way to elegance, and Cow Hollow, along with adjacent Pacific Heights, is replete with classic Victorian structures—gracious Queen Annes, perfectly trimmed Italianates, and vertiginous Stick-style town houses. By day, Cow Hollow's upscale Union Street bustles with well-heeled gallery goers and sushi lovers. At night the crowd grows younger and rowdier as the bars fill with partying patrons bent on showing that they know how to have a good time.

It was San Francisco's devotion to living well that inspired early city fathers to set aside a tract of western duneland in 1870 as an urban playground to rival New York's Central Park. Though the project was slow to take root, today the 1,017-acre Golden Gate Park is the largest cultivated city park in the country. Cyclists and inline skaters cruise the many paths that weave through verdant forests, delicately perfumed by the menthol of eucalyptus. Walkers can enjoy the sylvan coolness of the Strybing Arboretum, where more than 6,000 plant species from around the world thrive. A more subtle approach to landscape design characterizes the bonsai-fringed ponds, arching stone footbridge, and teahouse of the Japanese Tea Garden, built for the 1894 California Midwinter International Exposition. The fair was built around the park's broad, open Music Concourse, now rimmed by an eclectic array of museums. Among them is the Asian Art Museum, which features a stellar collection of Asian art ranging from Chinese bronzes to heavy stone sculptures from India's Jain period and Tibetan *thangkas* (scroll paintings).

The western edge of the park borders the Pacific and the stretch known as Ocean Beach. There is something wild and incongruous about this narrow strip of duneland located so close to the city proper. Long Pacific rollers blast the shore and seabirds scream in the wind. When the sun disappears in a blaze of colors, it has the force of alchemy, burnishing San Francisco in a wash of rosy gold. As the city falls into shadow, its streets and neighborhoods assume other guises, each distinctive and alluring and all waiting to be explored.

BAY AREA DELICACIES
Fisherman's Wharf, one of San Francisco's most popular tourist sites, is crowded with shops and eateries selling local specialties, including sourdough bread, fresh Dungeness crabs, and lobsters, left.

CITY LANDMARKS
San Francisco landmarks include the Columbus Tower (1905) and the Transamerica Pyramid (1971), far left, both well-known structures in the Financial District. The 855-foot pyramid, designed by William Pereira, is 48 stories high and capped by a 212-foot hollow spire. An observatory on the 27th floor is open to the public during business hours.

MONUMENTAL SPAN
After much controversy and the deaths of 10 workmen, the 1.7-mile Golden Gate Bridge, left, was finally completed in 1937. Anchored by twin 746-foot towers, the bright orange bridge carries some 120,000 motorists to and from Marin County and San Francisco each day. Walkers can reach the bridge via several access points located within the Golden Gate National Recreation Area.

Coit Tower, above, on Telegraph Hill, was built to honor San Francisco's volunteer fire-fighters. The money for the tower was willed to the city by Lillie Hitchcock Coit in the late 1920's.

OTHER SITES & ATTRACTIONS

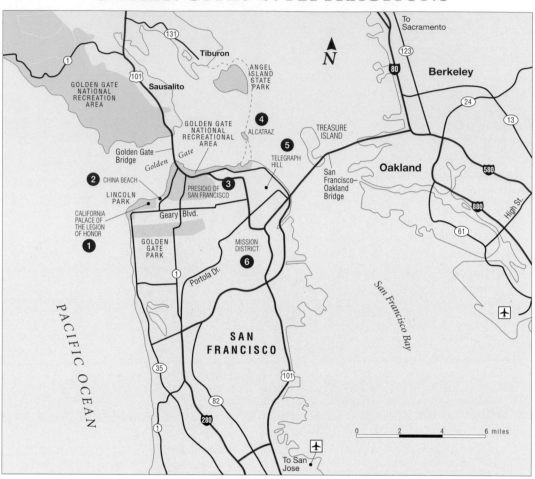

1 CALIFORNIA PALACE OF THE LEGION OF HONOR

Alma de Bretteville Spreckels had this replica of Paris' *Palais de la Legion d'Honneur* built in 1924 in honor of the soldiers from California who died in World War I. The palace also displays her extensive art collection. The colonnaded museum was designed by George Applegarth and built amid the windswept pines and cypresses of Lincoln Park. Renowned for its works by French sculptor Auguste Rodin (1840–1917), the museum also boasts a fine collection of French decorative arts and many important 18th- and 19th-century European paintings. Dance was a particular passion of Mrs. Spreckels and dance-related art is well represented in the museum. Located in Lincoln Park.

2 CHINA BEACH

Though water almost encircles San Francisco, the city offers surprisingly few good swimming areas, as ocean currents tend to be too strong for safety. This pocket-size beach, however, is both a safe spot for a cold dip in the Pacific and a pleasant place to have a picnic. Located at the end of Seacliff Avenue just west of the Presidio.

3 PRESIDIO OF SAN FRANCISCO

The Spanish built San Francisco's first European settlement—a military garrison, or presidio—on this site overlooking the Golden Gate in 1776. The Americans, under John C. Frémont, captured the fort in 1848 and continued to use it as a military installation. Budget cuts in 1994 brought the Presidio's soldiering days to an end. City fathers and environmentalists are still wrangling over the ultimate use of the lush, forested, 1,480-acre preserve, which is now part of the Golden Gate National Recreation Area. Visitors can examine displays of military memorabilia in the Presidio Museum and stroll along the Golden Gate Promenade to Fort Point, a pre–Civil War brick fortress that contains exhibits on American military life and history.

4 ALCATRAZ

The Rock, one of the United States' most notorious penitentiaries, was the forbidding, 12-acre island prison whose roster of inmates included such villains as Al Capone and Machine Gun Kelly. The island was named *Isla de los Alcatraces* (Island of the Pelicans) by Lt. Juan Manuel de Ayala, the first European to discover it, in 1775. It became a military prison during the Civil War and housed Native American prisoners during the opening of the

5 TELEGRAPH HILL

This tree-shaded summit rises 274 feet above the boisterous clamor of the North Beach neighborhood that was once the haunt of Beat Generation writers Jack Kerouac, Allen Ginsberg, and Lawrence Ferlinghetti. Originally a tower stood at the top of the peak, manned by an individual who would use semaphore signals to announce the arrival of a ship through the Golden Gate. Later, a telegraph system was installed on the hill to connect with Point Lobos in what is now Lincoln Park on the Pacific Coast. The hill's landmark is 210-foot-high Coit Tower. An elevator whisks visitors to the top, where they can view a panorama of the Bay area. A compelling Works Progress Administration mural of life in Depression-era California adorns the interior walls. Located in the north end of San Francisco.

6 MISSION DISTRICT

Founded in 1776 by Franciscan padres from Spain the city's oldest neighborhood is now home to people of many different cultures. Still, the area manages to cling tenaciously to its Latino ambience, particularly the section anchored by 24th St. The religious center of the community is Mission Dolores, the local name for Mission San Francisco de Asis, one in a chain of 21 missions established by Franciscan father Junipéro Serra in the late 1700's in what is now California. Original wooden reredos, imported from Mexico in 1796, are painted directly on the walls of the church's solid little stucco chapel, which is now dwarfed by a modern basilica. Located south of Market St.

French sculptor Auguste Rodin's The Thinker, left, is the centerpiece of the Court of Honor at the California Palace of the Legion of Honor. Casting of the 1912 statue was supervised by Rodin himself.

Southwest in the 1870's. Conscientious objectors were imprisoned here during World War I. From 1934 to 1963 it served as a federal maximum-security prison for almost 1,500 civilian criminals. Today Alcatraz is open to visitors, who arrive by ferry to tour its dank cell house and admire the flocks of seabirds, including black-crowned night herons, which roost amid the ruins. Located a mile and a half off San Francisco's north shore.

Each year more than 1 million visitors tour the empty, dilapidated buildings on Alcatraz Island, left, which served as a federal penitentiary from 1934–63. From 1969–71 the island was occupied by a group of Native Americans who wanted to draw attention to the plight of their people. Today it is under the jurisdiction of the National Park Service.

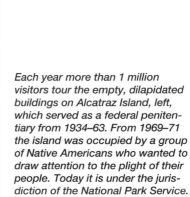

SEATTLE

This dynamic city makes apparent the exuberant and forward-looking spirit of its founders.

Seattle's skyscrapers rise through a morning mist, welcoming workday passengers aboard the Bainbridge Island ferry. As the vessel docks at Pier 52, ramps clunk into place, motors rumble to life, and cars pour off the boat. Nearby cranes load cargo ships. Trucks thunder along the Alaskan Way Viaduct. And Seattle begins another busy day. The city has always had a flair for enterprise, and the office towers that are the fruit of its labors are offset by parks and a multitude of outdoor artwork. Surrounded by the natural beauty of Puget Sound, Seattle toasts its prosperity with uniquely Northwestern panache.

The city of Seattle got off to a slow start, but from its earliest days its citizens displayed enormous optimism and energy. In 1851 the first white settlers—a party of 22 people led by a young man from Illinois named Arthur Denny—landed their boats on Alki Point in what is now West Seattle. They built their homes on the bluffs of today's downtown, above the calm waters of Elliott Bay.

In March 1852, another settler—and Denny's rival as the town leader—joined the battle to make Seattle a great city. David Swinson "Doc" Maynard

PICTURESQUE MARINA
Elliott Bay Marina, above, located at the base of Magnolia Bluff, has 1,200 slips that are divided between power craft and sailboats.

SEATTLE TALISMAN
Overleaf: The Space Needle soars above another famous Seattle landmark: Alexander Liberman's Olympic Iliad *(1984). The painted red steel sculpture measures 45 feet in height and 60 feet in length. Liberman, who uses industrially manufactured materials in his works, is also the creator of* Iliad, *a sculpture composed of huge gas storage tanks. The* Iliad *is on display at the Storm King Art Center in Mountainville, New York.*

set up a general store in the fledgling hamlet. Maynard played a key role in Seattle's development by naming the city, planning its street layout, and founding many of its businesses.

The Civil War, however, distracted the nation from its dreams of developing the West, and economic depressions and the Indian Wars deterred many prospective immigrants. But Seattle's sluggish growth failed to dim the settlers' optimism. Denny, although considered cold and unpleasant by many of his peers, began a successful brick factory and a real estate company. Amid muddy wagon ruts and the stumps of a freshly cleared forest, Denny donated the land for the first building of what would become the University of Washington.

Finally, in the 1880's, the westward surge began in earnest and immigrants arrived like a summer rain—at first in drops, then in torrents. The population of Seattle jumped from roughly 3,500 in 1880 to nearly 240,000 just 30 years later. Almost overnight the city had become the economic powerhouse of the region, with its prosperous banks and the roaring din of factories, foundries, shipyards, lumber mills, and canneries.

SYMBOL OF BOOM TIME

Today Seattle's Pioneer Square, with its many restored redbrick buildings, is a symbol of the city's boom era. This renovated historic district is a thriving place of art galleries, restaurants, and shops, interspersed with fountains and terraced gardens. The Great Fire of 1889 destroyed what would become about 33

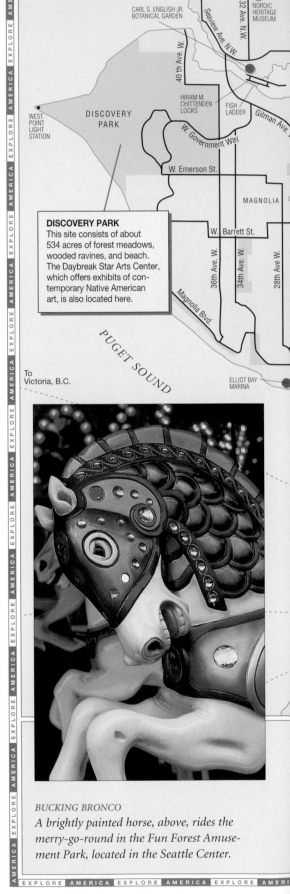

DISCOVERY PARK
This site consists of about 534 acres of forest meadows, wooded ravines, and beach. The Daybreak Star Arts Center, which offers exhibits of contemporary Native American art, is also located here.

BUCKING BRONCO
A brightly painted horse, above, rides the merry-go-round in the Fun Forest Amusement Park, located in the Seattle Center.

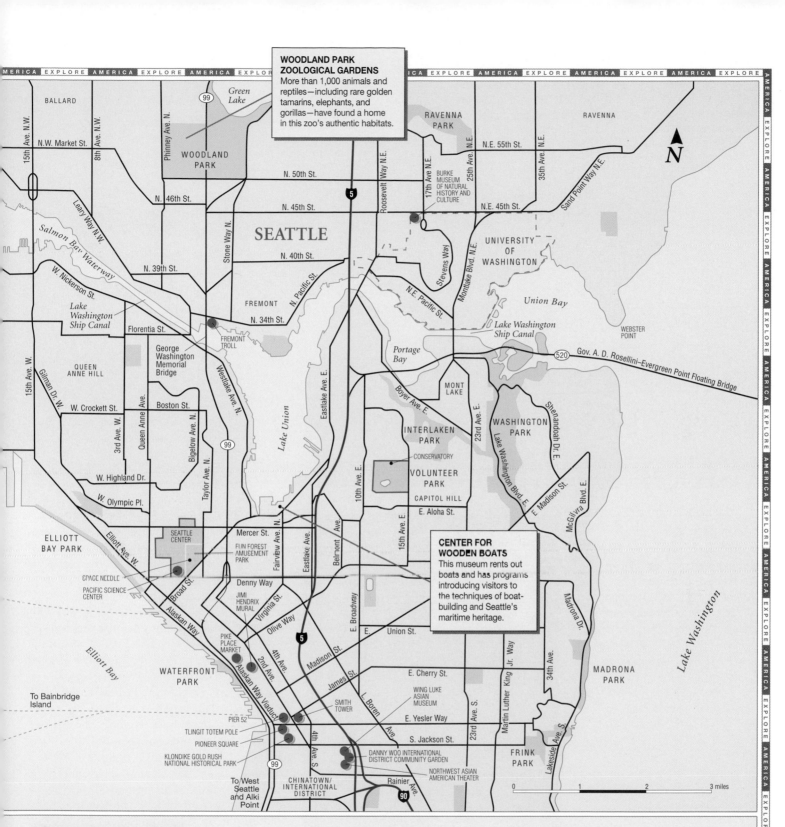

WOODLAND PARK ZOOLOGICAL GARDENS
More than 1,000 animals and reptiles—including rare golden tamarins, elephants, and gorillas—have found a home in this zoo's authentic habitats.

CENTER FOR WOODEN BOATS
This museum rents out boats and has programs introducing visitors to the techniques of boat-building and Seattle's maritime heritage.

SEATTLE

BALLARD
Green Lake
99
RAVENNA PARK
RAVENNA

15th Ave. N.W.
8th Ave. N.W.
N.W. Market St.
Phinney Ave. N.
WOODLAND PARK
N.E. 55th St.
25th Ave. N.E.
35th Ave. N.E.
Sand Point Way N.E.

N. 50th St.
5
Roosevelt Way N.E.
17th Ave N.E.
BURKE MUSEUM OF NATURAL HISTORY AND CULTURE
N.E. 45th St.

N. 46th St.
N. 45th St.
UNIVERSITY OF WASHINGTON

Leary Way N.W.
Salmon Bay Waterway
Stone Way N.
N. 40th St.
Stevens Way
Montlake Blvd. N.E.

W. Nickerson St.
N. 39th St.
N. Pacific St.
Union Bay
WEBSTER POINT

Lake Washington Ship Canal
FREMONT
N. 34th St.
N.E. Pacific St.
Lake Washington Ship Canal

Florentia St.
FREMONT TROLL
Portage Bay
520
Gov. A. D. Rosellini—Evergreen Point Floating Bridge

George Washington Memorial Bridge
Westlake Ave. N.
Boyer Ave. E.
MONT LAKE

QUEEN ANNE HILL
W. Crockett St.
99
Eastlake Ave. E.
INTERLAKEN PARK
WASHINGTON PARK
Shenandoah Dr. E.

Gilman Dr. W.
3rd Ave. W.
Queen Anne Ave.
Boston St.
Bigelow Ave. N.
Taylor Ave. N.
Lake Union
CONSERVATORY
Lake Washington Blvd. E.
E. Madison St.
McGilvra Blvd. E.

W. Highland Dr.
VOLUNTEER PARK

W. Olympic Pl.
10th Ave. E.
CAPITOL HILL
E. Aloha St.

ELLIOTT BAY PARK
Elliott Ave. W.
SEATTLE CENTER
Mercer St.
Fairview Ave. N.
Eastlake Ave.
Belmont Ave.
15th Ave. E.

FUN FOREST AMUSEMENT PARK
SPACE NEEDLE
PACIFIC SCIENCE CENTER
Broad St.
Denny Way
Madrona Dr.

Alaskan Way
JIMI HENDRIX MURAL
Virginia St.
Olive Way
5
E. Broadway
E. Union St.

Elliott Bay
PIKE PLACE MARKET
2nd Ave.
4th Ave.
Madison St.
E. Cherry St.
MADRONA PARK

WATERFRONT PARK
Alaskan Way Viaduct
James St.
WING LUKE ASIAN MUSEUM
34th Ave.
Lake Washington

To Bainbridge Island
PIER 52
SMITH TOWER
L. Boren Ave.
E. Yesler Way
23rd Ave. S.
Martin Luther King Jr. Way

TLINGIT TOTEM POLE
PIONEER SQUARE
4th Ave. S.
S. Jackson St.
FRINK PARK
Lakeside Ave. S.

KLONDIKE GOLD RUSH NATIONAL HISTORICAL PARK
99
DANNY WOO INTERNATIONAL DISTRICT COMMUNITY GARDEN
NORTHWEST ASIAN AMERICAN THEATER

To West Seattle and Alki Point
CHINATOWN/INTERNATIONAL DISTRICT
Rainier Ave.
90

0   1   2   3 miles

INFORMATION FOR VISITORS

I-90, the major east–west route, crosses the Cascade Mountains and approaches Seattle from Spokane. I-5 provides north–south access from the Canadian border. The Seattle-Tacoma International Airport is located midway between Seattle and Tacoma on Hwy. 99. Amtrak provides rail service to King Street Station. Greyhound buses arrive at the terminal at 8th Ave. and Stewart St., and Trailways at the terminal of Westlake Ave. Seattle operates a network of trolleys and buses that makes it easy to travel around the city. The avenues run in a north–south direction; streets run east–west. Water-related events dominate Seattle's social calendar, and include the Maritime Festival in May, Seafair in July, the Salmon Homecoming in September, and the Argosy Christmas Ship Festival at Yuletide. Summer temperatures average about 70°F, and in winter they rarely drop below 32°F. For more information: Seattle/King County Convention and Visitors Bureau, 520 Pike St., Suite 1300, Seattle, WA 98101; 206-461-5807.

ERICA EXPLORE AMERICA EXPLORE AMERICA EXPLORE AMERICA EXPLORE AMERICA EXPLORE AMERICA EXPLORE AMERICA EXPLORE AMERICA EXPLORE AMERICA EXPLORE AMERICA EXPLORE AMERICA EXPLORE A

SEATTLE 111

HEART AND SOUL
Pike Place Market, above, is one of the oldest continuously working public markets in the nation. For many residents it represents the heart and soul of Seattle. An estimated 9 million people shop here every year. Some come for hard-to-find items, others for the showmanship of its seasoned vendors, and still others to enjoy the ambience.

SIXTIES ICON
A vibrant mural of Seattle-born Jimi Hendrix, right, transforms a downtown wall. His father bought him his first guitar from Meyer's Music, a music store that once stood at this spot.

blocks of Pioneer Square, virtually the entire business district. The area, originally an island bordering a tidal flat, had always suffered poor drainage because of its low elevation. The fire created an opportunity to rebuild at a higher level. The new brick and stone buildings, however, were built at the original elevation—the streets were raised with landfill. Eventually hollow sidewalks were bridged over to the buildings from elevated streets, at the second, or sometimes third, floor. The original ground floors are now, in fact, underground.

In 1893 the Great Northern Railroad linked Seattle with the rest of the nation. With its aggressive business acumen and robust economy, the city was poised to take advantage of a windfall: the discovery of gold on the Klondike tributary of Alaska's Yukon River. On July 17, 1897, the steamer *Portland* docked at the Seattle waterfront carrying 68 miners and two tons of gold. The news spread like wildfire, and overnight thousands of men began streaming through Seattle in search of instant wealth. The Klondike Gold Rush National Historical Park, housed in the old Union Trust Annex, uses film and pictures to tell the story not only of gold fever, but also of its profitable effect on Seattle, the chief supplier and departure point for many money-minded adventurers heading to the North.

Although the miners' luck soon waned, Seattle's endured. The city constructed ships for the Spanish-American War and captured lucrative Asian markets, trading timber and salmon for silk, tea, and hemp. Seattle was a brash young city, and its citizens considered no challenge too ambitious. A testament to Seattle's upstart mood, the resplendent pearl-hued Smith Tower stands at the corner of Second Avenue and Yesler Way in Pioneer Square. When completed in 1914, its 42 floors made it the tallest building in the world outside Manhattan, and it may still be the most beloved building in the city. The quirky Chinese Temple Room on the 35th floor is a popular wedding site and has one of the best views in town.

The Chinatown/International District is the cultural and commercial center for Seattle's Asian population. The community is largely made up of Asian-Americans of Vietnamese, Chinese, Japanese, Korean, and Filipino descent. Many of their ancestors arrived here seeking a haven from poverty and war in their homelands, or from racial persecution elsewhere in America. They labored on railroads, farms, and in the fishing industry. Many of them prospered, purchased land, and started businesses of their own. Such landmark family operations as the Tsue Chong Noodle Company and Yick Fung Import Bazaar attest to the fact that determination and hard work breed success.

Today many elderly residents practice their time-honored horticultural magic in the Danny Woo International District Community Garden, while members of the younger generations experiment

SLOW DEVELOPER
When the first settlers arrived on Alki Point in 1851, they named it New York. But when its growth proved too slow, area residents renamed the point Alki, a Native American word meaning "by and by." The first light on Alki Point was a brass kerosene lantern that was hung on the side of a barn in 1887. After the Seattle/Port Blakely passenger steamer Dix collided with the schooner Jeanie in 1910, killing 39 people, the government agreed to build a lighthouse here. Alki Point Light, left, is now automated and uses a 500-watt electric lightbulb that lasts about 3,900 hours.

with new modes of expression at the Northwest Asian American Theater. The Wing Luke Asian Museum on Seventh Street, in the heart of the International District, weaves together the ethnically diverse strands of the neighborhood. Changing exhibits present works by contemporary Asian-American artists. More than a touchstone of the past, this museum is a launching pad to the com-munity's future, addressing issues affecting Asian-Americans while expanding its focus to include such recent arrivals as Pacific Islanders and Hmong tribespeople from Southeast Asia.

For all its industriousness, Seattle has always known how to enjoy its prosperity. Capitol Hill, along with Belmont Historic District, and so-called Millionaire's Row are enclaves of Victorian, Tudor,

LEGENDS OF A WOMAN WARRIOR
A Tlingit totem pole, above, at First Avenue and Yesler Way, commem-orates a Tlingit leader named Chief-of-All-Women, who drowned in Alaska's Nass River on the way to care for her ill sister. The totem pole is a copy of one that was taken from the front of the leader's lineage house at Tongass, Alaska, by a group of businessmen in 1899. Each of the offenders was fined $500. The original totem pole was carved from hemlock wood. However, it was damaged by fire and rot and replaced in 1938 with a duplicate carved in more durable red cedar.

and Georgian homes that once belonged to Seattle's turn-of-the-century elite. Volunteer Park, a trim, manicured green space from the belle epoque, is a natural counterpoint to the elegant architecture that lines the streets of these districts. On languid summer evenings, music from the enormous bandstand wafts through the park's spruce and cherry trees. In the conservatory, a glass pavilion inspired by London's Crystal Palace, orchids and other tropical exotics beguile the senses. To the west, when weather permits, the view extends from the teeming Seattle core across Puget Sound to the jagged spires of the Olympic Mountains.

HISTORIC MARKET

After soaking up the atmosphere of Volunteer Park, visitors should take the time to view the sights at the Pike Place Market. At the turn of the century, Seattle's markets were in the hands of commerce agents who paid the farmers very little and charged the public exorbitant prices; the agents often destroyed surpluses to keep prices high. In August 1907 the city's residents rebelled, declaring a market day so that local farmers could sell directly to consumers. Only a dozen farmers, all of them Japanese or Italian, showed up, but the seed had been planted. Word spread quickly, and by the end of that first week hundreds of farm wagons loaded with produce were parked along the bluff. Three months later the first permanent covered stalls went up, and a Seattle tradition was born. At times there were threats of closing this popular attraction—the most recent coming in the late 1960's, when the market risked facing the wrecking ball to make room for an urban renewal project. Happily, in 1971 a citizens' group was able to save the market by securing its designation as a National Historic District.

Today Pike Place Market has expanded beyond its founders' wildest expectations. Halibut and salmon are offered for sale by enthusiastic stallkeepers and vegetables are still trucked here from inland farms. Stalls selling blown-glass objects and jewelry are tucked between booths selling locally produced honey. In May the Pike Place Market Festival offers free performances on three stages, while clowns and street musicians stroll through the market, entertaining the public.

The market has outgrown its original housing and now occupies neighboring buildings, where specialty shops are packed to the rafters with an eclectic array of Tibetan herbs, umbrellas, cheeses, hats, books, crumpets, live parrots, chocolates, and knives. German vendors sell their wares alongside Jamaicans, Filipinos, and Greeks. The clientele, too, is every bit as diverse. Virtually everybody shops here, creating an extraordinarily varied atmosphere of lifestyles and ethnicities.

Seattle is a city of water. In fact, part of its mystique is the way water subtly unites the area's diverse inhabitants. This is especially true along the Lake Washington Ship Canal—an engineering marvel that links Puget Sound with Lake Union and Lake Washington. Completed in 1917 after some 60 years of dreams, speeches, and studies, the water-

TUMBLING TREASURE
The Waterfall Garden, below, in the Pioneer Square Historic District, was laid out on the site where James E. Casey, a Seattle resident and founder of the United Parcel Service, established his messenger business in 1907.

IMPOSING FACADE
The Gothic-style Suzzallo Library of the University of Washington, left, completed in the 1920's, was designed by local architect Carl Gould. Since then, the library has grown considerably, requiring numerous renovations and additions, which took place in the 1930's, 1960's, and 1990's. The library's arched windows let light into the main reading room, a cathedral-like area that offers students and faculty a quiet sanctuary in which to read and study.

Pioneer Square's Klondike Gold Rush National Historical Park Visitor Center, right, offers slide shows, tours, and films depicting the life of miners during the gold rush days of 1898. The visitor center represents the southernmost post of the national historical park, which commemorates the miners' route to Skagway, Alaska.

BEETLEMANIA
An immense concrete troll, below, poised to devour the Volkswagen Beetle it holds in its hand, lurks under the north end of the Aurora Bridge in the Fremont District. The sculpture, known as the Fremont Troll, *was created by artists Steve Badanes, Will Martin, Donna Walter, and Ross Whitehead.*

way slices across the isthmus north of downtown and provides access to the sea for inland industries and recreation facilities. Distinctive neighborhoods line the canal, including the floating communities of Lake Union. Houseboats have been a feature of Seattle's waterfront life since at least the Klondike gold rush, providing a place for the poor to live cheaply. Today designer houseboats are home to artists and accountants. Across the Montlake Cut lies the University of Washington. The site of Arthur Denny's humble schoolhouse is now occupied by the Burke Museum of Natural History and Culture, which pays tribute to the Pacific Northwest Indians with a superb collection of dugout canoes.

Neighboring Fremont, another neighborhood along the canal, is a bohemian quarter full of eclectic shops, alternative bistros, and some of Seattle's more iconoclastic sculptures, including Richard Beyer's *Waiting for the Interurban*—a group portrait decorated by locals to commemorate everything from Christmas to the upcoming prom. In nearby Ballard, blue eyes, clipped accents, and a proliferation of Volvos hint at a Scandinavian influence and the Nordic Heritage Museum confirms it. This unique institution—the only museum in the nation devoted to the cultures of all five Nordic countries—recounts the saga of the immigrants' odyssey and explores their contribution to American life. Exquisite hand-crafted objects on display range from a full-scale Viking ship to hand-painted boxes and folkloric costumes. Scandinavians arrived in Ballard in the late 19th and early 20th centuries. Although poor, they possessed valuable woodworking and seafaring skills. As master carpenters, boatbuilders, and fishermen, they became indispensable to Seattle's prosperity.

Water is also the big attraction at the Hiram M. Chittenden Locks, situated on the Lake Washington Ship Canal. At this popular spot, visitors can watch a procession of ships and boats go by—as many as 80,000 a year. The locks, which were the second-largest in the Americas when built (only the locks of the Panama Canal were larger), are an ingenious system that raises and lowers boats anywhere from 6 to 20 feet, depending on the tides. A barrier separates salt water from freshwater, thereby preserving the upstream environment. The U.S. Army Corps of Engineers, who completed the locks and the dam in 1917, realized that their construction would keep the salmon from returning via Lake Washington to the lakes, rivers, or streams where they were born in order to spawn. As a result, they installed a network of weirs and pools on the southern bank. Visitors can watch the salmon negotiating the fish ladder through underwater windows.

Like Pike Place Market, the locks bring together a pageant of people: sailors waving from barges,

affluent yachtsmen, fishermen on trawlers, and kayakers. Flanked by the lovely Carl S. English Jr. Botanical Garden, the area is an ideal place for visitors to picnic and stroll along the pathways as they watch the boats move through the locks.

SEATTLE CENTER

A sleek monorail whisks passengers from downtown to the Seattle Center, located about a mile away. The futuristic tram established the city in the minds of many as the gateway to the future. The Seattle Center, a complex of buildings set on the 1962 World's Fair grounds, is the home of an innovative opera company, four regional theaters, and several professional sports teams, including the high-flying basketball team, the Seattle SuperSonics. Situated at the center of the 74-acre landscaped campus are the shops and restaurants of the Seattle Center House. Also on the campus, although adminis- tered separately, is the Pacific Science Center, built for the 1962 World's Fair and the first science and technology museum to be established in the nation. Exhibits range from "Dinosaurs: A Journey through Time" to "Tech Zone" and "Waterworks."

The enduring symbol of the fair and the city of Seattle is the 605-foot-tall Space Needle, designed by architects John Graham and Victor Steinbrueck. From the observation deck, Seattle's unique geography becomes apparent. The city is surrounded by tentacles of land and sea and locked in the briny embrace of Puget Sound. Rumpled hills, verdant parklands, and azure lakes complete the picture. To the southeast rises Mount Rainier; to the west the Olympic Mountains seem to touch the sky. From the Space Needle's dizzying perch, it is easy to imagine why the city's founders held on to their dream, knowing that sooner or later Seattle—a city with one foot in the past and the other stepping toward the future—would come into its own.

SEASIDE VISTA
Viewed from Elliott Bay
Waterfront, Seattle's skyline,
above, shows off its crisp lines.

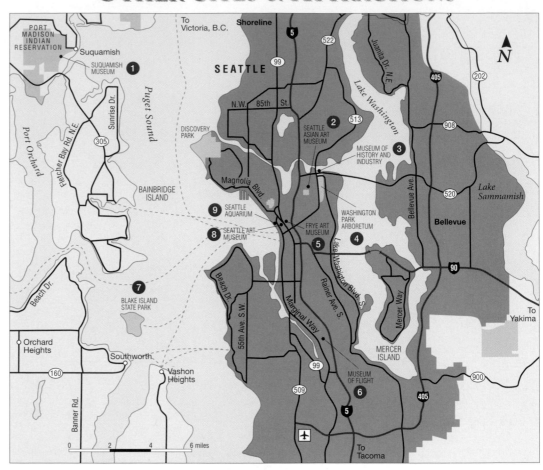

Thirty aircraft are on display in the Museum of Flight's Great Gallery, below, including a DC-3, a 1929 Boeing Model 80A-1, and a 1953 Grumman F9F-8 Cougar.

① SUQUAMISH MUSEUM

The Suquamish Museum displays artifacts that help visitors understand the culture of the region's Native American inhabitants. The museum's premier exhibits are "The Eyes of Chief Seattle," an award-winning exhibition focusing on tribal craft and spiritu-ality, and "Comes Forth Laughing, Voices of the Suquamish People," a multimedia presentation that uses oral history and historic photographs to recount the Suquamish's effort to preserve their identity in the 20th century. Every third weekend of August the powwow circuit arrives in the nearby town of Suquamish for Chief Seattle Days, a festival that includes traditional dances, salmon bakes, and canoe races. Located off Hwy. 305 on the Port Madison Indian Reservation.

② SEATTLE ASIAN ART MUSEUM

This 1933 Art Moderne masterpiece, which is situated in beautiful Volunteer Park, contains one of the five most significant collections of Japanese art in the world. The museum also has rotating exhibitions of its vast collection of Chinese ceramics, some of which are more than 7,000 years old. Art of the Himalayas, India, and Southeast Asia complete the displays. The KADO Tea Garden is a popular place to sip tea and contemplate the art of the Orient. Located at 1400 E. Prospect St.

③ MUSEUM OF HISTORY AND INDUSTRY

This museum, located on the shores of Lake Washington, concentrates on the daily life of Seattle from the 1850's onward. Based on an extensive

118

collection of photographs, the museum's exhibit subjects range from the Great Fire of 1889 to the fishing and logging industries. Another collection of photographs shows the backstage preparations for ballet and opera performances. The museum offers summer walking tours through various Seattle locales. Located at 2700 24th Ave. E.

4 WASHINGTON PARK ARBORETUM

This sprawling 200-acre urban refuge was created at the turn of the century as a haven for the wealthy residents of the area. Today everyone is welcome to meander through the park's wooded glades and demonstration gardens, and stroll along promenades blossoming with azaleas. Seattle's temperate climate encourages the growth of a wide variety of plants, including camellias, hollies, and Japanese maples. The park's walks are linked to the Montlake Cut National Scenic Waterside Trail. Located at 2300 Arboretum Dr. E.

5 FRYE ART MUSEUM

Situated on First Hill, once Seattle's Millionaire's Row, this state-of-the-art museum contains a collection of 19th- and 20th-century European and American paintings that were assembled by Seattle pioneers Charles and Emma Frye. Reflecting the Fryes' heritage, the collection displays a strong bias toward paintings by German artists—but also contains masterpieces by such American artists as Homer, Whistler, and Wyeth, as well as paintings by Picasso and other European artists. The museum is noted for its changing contemporary arts exhibits. The new auditorium hosts lectures, films, and jazz concerts. In keeping with the Fryes' philosophy that art should be accessible to everyone, admission to the museum is free. Located at 704 Terry Ave.

6 MUSEUM OF FLIGHT

Listed on the National Register of Historic Places, the largest air and space museum on the West Coast occupies the site of Seattle's first powered airplane flight in 1910. The museum incorporates the original Boeing plant, called the Red Barn, which displays early biplanes and a re-creation of an early airplane manufacturing shop. Fifty distinctive planes fill the barn and the adjacent Great Gallery. These include the human-powered *Gossamer Albatross,* a Lockheed Blackbird spy plane, and NASA's 1968 Apollo command module. The highlight of the museum's innovative interactive exhibits is the three-story air traffic control tower, where visitors can listen in on actual flight communications from adjacent Boeing Field. Located at 9404 E. Marginal Way S.

7 BLAKE ISLAND STATE PARK

Chartered ferries shuttle visitors to this wooded 476-acre gem in Puget Sound. Seattle's impressive skyline is only eight miles away, but the island's many waterfront trails seem a world apart. Blake Island is reputed to be the birthplace of the famed Native chief Sealth, or Seattle, who was a 19th-century chief of the Suquamish and Duwamish peoples. The island is now home to Tillicum Village, where North Coast Indian traditions are brought to life. The village offers guests a traditional meal of steamed clams and nectar, along with salmon baked over an alder fire and served in a cedar longhouse. Visitors can also see stage shows that use dance, music, and costumes to celebrate Suquamish heritage. Tours to Blake Island depart from Pier 55/56.

8 SEATTLE ART MUSEUM

Designed by post-Modernist architect Robert Venturi, the Seattle Art Museum epitomizes the city's affectionately irreverent approach to high culture. The building is playful in design and the eclectic collection ranges from African ceremonial masks and Northwest Indian fabrics to moody tableaus by Edward Hopper. Also on display are several paintings by offbeat local artists. Located at 100 University St.

9 SEATTLE AQUARIUM

The pride of Seattle's aquarium is its large undersea dome, which offers visitors a fish-eye view of a fascinating marine world of Puget Sound. More than 400 animal species, including the giant Pacific octopus, bright billed puffins, and sleek sea otters dwell in the aquarium. The highlight of an exhibit on the fragile tropical ecosystem of a Pacific Ocean coral roof is watching the aquarium's black tipped reef sharks. Each September the aquarium hosts the Salmon Homecoming, a popular festival that celebrates the region's most important marine resource and cultural icon. Events range from a salmon bake, a three-and-a-half mile run, a powwow, and Native American cultural performances. Located at Waterfront Park at Pier 59.

Visitors to the Seattle Aquarium, above, gaze at the waters of Puget Sound through the windows of the aquarium's Underwater Dome.

A blossoming Japanese cherry tree, below, arches over a pathway in the Japanese Garden, located within Washington Park Arboretum.

Battery houses at White Point Gardens, Charleston, South Carolina.

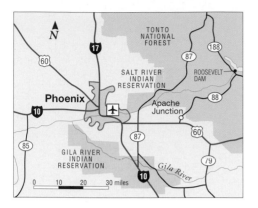

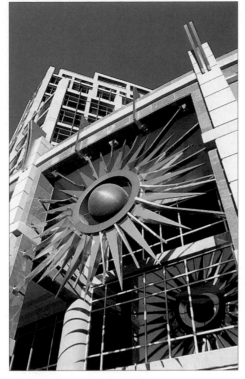

Phoenix's new city hall, left, designed by Langdon Wilson Architects, was completed in 1994. Jack Black's copper and steel sculpture, known as the Sunburst, adorns its facade.

Like the mythical bird that rose from its own ashes, the city of Phoenix emerged from the ruins of the Hohokam civilization that flourished in Arizona between the 8th and 14th centuries. Established in 1870, Phoenix has grown from a cluster of adobe dwellings to a gleaming metropolis that ranks as the largest city in Arizona and the sixth-largest in the nation.

The city began as a farming community whose irrigation system was based on the network of canals built by the Hohokam. This tribe of desert farmers tamed the Salt River as early as 300 B.C., channeling its waters to grow crops of beans, corn, squash, and cotton. They tilled the soil for at least 1,700 years, only to disappear mysteriously in A.D. 1450. Visitors can tour the remains of a 13th-century Hohokam community in Phoenix's Pueblo Grande Museum and Cultural Park, which includes excavations of Hohokam canals and an oval depression similar to the ball courts found in ancient ruins in Mexico. A reconstructed pueblo room displays Hohokam artifacts.

As 19th-century farmers capitalized on the region's agricultural potential, Phoenix became the supply center for mining towns that soon sprouted in the ore-laden hills of north-central Arizona. The state's frontier days are re-created at the Pioneer Arizona Living History Museum, where costumed interpreters perform tasks in a village of 26 buildings that date from 1861 to 1912. The site includes a school, church, sheriff's office, blacksmith's shop, and the John Sears House, the first frame house in town.

With the arrival of the railroad in 1887, the citizens of Phoenix imported wood to build ornate Victorian houses, some of which still stand in Heritage and Science

Park. The wraparound veranda and hexagonal turret of the Rosson House recall the architecture of early Phoenix. Built for the mayor in 1895, the restored mansion features parquet floors, pressed-tin ceilings, a carved staircase, and period furnishings.

SPUR TO GREATNESS
The Roosevelt Dam, dedicated in 1911, ensured water for Phoenix's continued growth. Later, the advent of air conditioning spurred industrial development and the city experienced a population boom; today, 1.2 million people reside here.

Although the city is forward-looking, it also maintains strong ties to its past. At The Heard Museum visitors can view a world-class collection of Southwest Indian artifacts, including the clothing, jewelry, tools, and weapons of such regional tribes as the Navajo, Hopi, and Zuni. Visitors can also climb 2,608-foot-high Squaw Peak for a bird's-eye view of the city and then head over to the Desert Botanical Garden in Papago Park to take a stroll through the garden's vast array of native vegetation, including paloverde, mesquite, and ocotillo trees — all typical of the Southwest.

Phoenix and the surrounding area boast an average of 300 days of sunshine a year. The city has more than 150 golf courses, which attract golfers from all over the nation. More than a dozen suburbs sprawl across the Valley of the Sun. Visitors can take Jeep rides into Scottsdale and Carefree, go hot-air ballooning over the valley, or marvel at the colorful desert scenery during flight-seeing tours to the Grand Canyon.

FOR MORE INFORMATION:
Phoenix and Valley of the Sun Convention and Visitors Bureau, One Arizona Center, 400 E. Van Buren St., Suite 600, Phoenix, AZ 85004-2290; 602-254-6500.

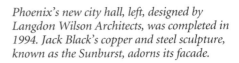

The territorial capital of Arizona was moved from Prescott to Phoenix in 1889, and in 1900 the territorial legislature opened the Old State Capitol, left. Now the State Capitol Museum, the building houses material relating to state history, including a scale model of the battleship U.S.S. Arizona *and the document that proclaimed Arizona the 48th state in 1912.*

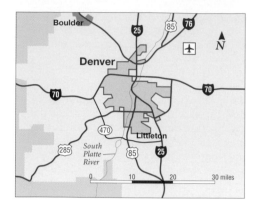

The Denver Botanic Gardens, located a short walk from the Denver Museum of Natural History, has a conservatory, right, which contains an award-winning collection of orchids.

I n 1858 the gleam of gold lured fortune hunters to the confluence of the South Platte River and Cherry Creek, where the Rocky Mountains rear skyward from the vastness of the Great Plains. The gold soon played out, but the little town of Denver grew and prospered, especially after prospectors discovered rich veins of silver in the nearby mountains. Although coal, oil shale, uranium, and natural gas have replaced gold and silver, mining still plays an important part in the economy of the Mile High City.

Visitors to the city's 16th Street Mall can sense the prosperity of this thriving city. This mile-long pedestrian area, created in the 1980's, is a mecca for shoppers and

Downtown's Cubist profile forms a modern backdrop to Civic Center Park, below, one of Denver's more than 200 city parks and the home of Colorado's state capitol.

strollers. Free shuttle buses run the length of the mall. At nearby Larimer Square— one of the city's more than 20 historic districts—shops and restaurants occupy brick buildings that were erected between 1870 and 1890. At one end of the mall stands the sandstone Brown Palace Hotel, a Denver landmark since it opened its doors in 1892. Wrought-iron balconies surround its nine-story atrium, which is topped by spectacular Tiffany stained-glass skylights.

ONE OF A KIND
At the southeastern end of 16th Street Mall rises the golden dome of the Colorado state capitol. Modeled on the U.S. Capitol, the building boasts interior walls made of rose onyx. The onyx was mined south of Denver near the town of Beulah, the world's only known source of this mineral. Its supply was exhausted by the construction. For spectacular views of the city and the mountains, visitors can climb the 93 steps to the top of the rotunda. The 13th step of the capitol's west exterior stairway is exactly one mile above sea level.

A short walk from the capitol and 16th Street Mall lies the U.S. Mint. The mint's stamping machines turn out all denominations, including some $1.5 million worth of nickel-alloy pennies each day. The mint

was established in 1860 by prospectors Emanuel Gruber and Austin Clark to process locally mined gold dust and nuggets into bars. Daily tours take visitors through the facility, which is housed in a 1904 Italian Renaissance–style building.

At the Denver Museum of Natural History—the seventh-largest museum in the nation—visitors can view Colorado's wealth of dinosaur fossils and skeletons. In the Colorado History Museum they can see dioramas and exhibits that trace the impact made on the region by Indians, explorers, gold miners, pioneers, and cowboys. Native American art is exhibited in a Modernist home at the Denver Art Museum, which also displays ceremonial clothes from the South Pacific, ancient Greek statuary, and works by Picasso, Braque, and Matisse. The Black American West Museum and Heritage Center, housed in the home of Dr. Justina Ford, Denver's first African-American physician, highlights the vital role played by African-Americans in the opening of the West. A distinctly Denver museum is the Molly Brown House, the residence of the "unsinkable" Molly Brown. The plucky widow of silver millionaire James J. Brown survived the sinking of the *Titanic* and became a national heroine for her efforts to help her lifeboat companions survive the ordeal.

FOR MORE INFORMATION:
Denver Convention and Visitors Bureau, 1555 California St., Suite 300, Denver, CO 80202-4264; 303-892-1112 or 800-393-8559.

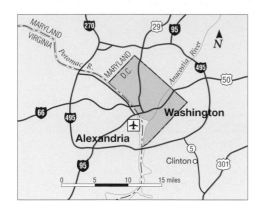

A swampy parcel of land lying near the juncture of the Potomac and Anacostia rivers was an unlikely spot to choose for a national capital. Nevertheless, this was the site selected by the United States Congress in 1790. Washington stands on 100 square miles of territory that was ceded by Virginia and Maryland and named the District of Columbia. Home of the federal government and a major cultural and educational center in its own right, the cosmopolitan city of Washington draws millions of visitors each year. It is a city where important issues are discussed and decisions are made. It is also a place that celebrates the nation's achievements and infinite possibilities.

L'ENFANT'S CITY

George Washington appointed Maj. Pierre Charles L'Enfant, a French military engineer, to lay out the city. L'Enfant drew on European ideas of urban planning to design a capital of wide avenues, spacious circles, and broad vistas. Sweeping diagonal streets provide a counterpoint to a basic grid street pattern. The centerpiece of the city's design is a wide mall, stretching westward from the Potomac to the Capitol Building.

The nation's lawmakers gather in the Capitol, which served as the symbolic center of Washington in L'Enfant's design and has been the seat of Congress since 1800. The building's dome, erected in the 1850's, rises above the rotunda, and is 180 feet high and 90 feet in diameter. The wings of the Capitol house the Senate and the House of Representatives.

Near the Capitol are two monuments dedicated to the written word: the Library of Congress and the Folger Library. The largest library in the world, the Library of Congress serves the needs of legislators and is also the national library; hour-long tours guide visitors through some of the library's collections, allowing them to view a Gutenberg Bible from A.D. 1450. The Folger Library is dedicated to the life and work of William Shakespeare and contains first-edition folios of his plays. Plays are presented in an Elizabethan-style theater.

On the National Mall, which stretches from the Capitol to the Lincoln Memorial, stands the monumental National Gallery of Art, dedicated to American and European master artists. Directly opposite the gallery's East Building is the National Air and Space Museum, with a collection charting the development of aircraft and the history of space flight. Both this museum and the National Gallery of Art are units of the Smithsonian Institution, affectionately called America's Attic. The Smithsonian administers 16 major museums from its headquarters, a building known as the Castle on the Mall. Other museums on the Mall include the National Museum of Natural History, the National Museum of American History, and the National Museum of African Art.

Roughly halfway down the Mall rises the 555.5-foot-high Washington Monument. The massive obelisk is the world's tallest masonry tower. Begun in 1848, it was not completed until 1884. Visitors can climb its 898 steps or take an elevator to the observation area, which provides panoramic views of the city. To the south of the monument, across the Tidal Basin, stands the circular domed rotunda erected in memory of Thomas Jefferson. To the west, the Reflecting Pool serenely extends to the Lincoln Memorial, which contains Daniel Chester French's renowned 19-foot-high statue of the 16th president.

Visitors remember the dead as they read the names of Americans engraved on the V-shaped Vietnam Veterans Memorial, near the Lincoln Memorial. Memory is also the theme of the U.S. Holocaust Memorial Museum, a dignified limestone-and-red-brick building that chronicles the mass killings carried out by Adolf Hitler and the Nazis from 1933 to 1945.

North of the Washington Monument lies the White House, which has been the residence of every U.S. president except George Washington. Designed by Irishman James Hoban, the building has been extensively modified over the years. Portions of the White House are open to the public; tours begin at the East Gate, which is located on East Executive Avenue.

FOR MORE INFORMATION:
Washington, D.C. Convention and Visitors Association, 1212 New York Ave. NW, Washington, DC 20005-3992; 202-789-7000.

The Capitol, below, is open daily for tours. Visitors can also obtain a pass from their senator or representative to watch sessions of Congress from special visitors' galleries.

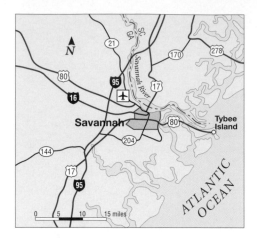

Savannah is home to a harmonious collection of more than 2,000 historic buildings, among them romantic mansions like the Gingerbread House, above, on Bull Street at 36th Street.

John Berendt, who wrote *Midnight in the Garden of Good and Evil*, called Savannah "luscious." In *Gone With the Wind*, Margaret Mitchell called it "that gently mannered city by the sea." Even its name is a word to linger over. A vital port and busy manufacturing center, Savannah evokes images of tree-lined streets and moody 18th-century squares graced with stone fountains and noble statues. Its two-square-mile Historic Landmark District, rescued from decay and imbued with new life, has become a major tourist attraction.

Today Savannah's gentle nature beguiles visitors who take the time to savor its moods and ponder its colorful past.

PLANNED CITY

Perched on a bluff above the Savannah River 17 miles from the Atlantic, Savannah was founded by Gen. James Oglethorpe, who brought a party of 114 colonists up the river in 1733. Oglethorpe planned the city based on a series of wards, or neighborhoods, each of which was built around a square. These squares are now planted with live oaks and azaleas and often incorporate statuary and fountains.

Savannah prospered through slavery and the export of cotton. In 1793 Eli Whitney invented the cotton gin on a plantation not far from Savannah; his invention quickly turned cotton into a booming business and made the city wealthy. The nexus of the cotton trade was Savannah's riverfront, lined with the brick offices and warehouses of the cotton factors, or agents. Today these restored 19th-century structures do duty as restaurants, pubs, and specialty shops. Catwalks link the rear of these buildings with the top of the bluff and the Bay Street Promenade. In between lies Factors Walk, a picturesque cobbled lane that preserves the atmosphere of the cotton-dealing days.

Savannah woke up to its heritage in 1957 when a group of local women banded together to save the 1815 Federal-style Davenport House from demolition. They founded the groundbreaking Historic Savannah Foundation, which over the years has been responsible for saving more than 1,700 historic buildings, including the 1819 Owens-Thomas House on Oglethorpe

Square and Lafayette Square's Andrew Low House, built in 1819 on the site of a jail. The latter, a graceful Georgian house, was once the home of Juliette Low, who founded the Girl Scouts of the U.S.A. in 1912.

When Gen. William T. Sherman marched into Savannah in December 1864 during his March to the Sea, he was so taken with the city that he spared it the fiery fate of Atlanta. He set up his local headquarters in the 1853 Green-Meldrim House on Madison Square. The house was built in the Gothic Revival style, and its wrought-iron porch is typical of the decorative ironwork favored by wealthy residents of the period.

In contrast to the grandeur of Savannah's house museums, the modest King-Tisdell Cottage interprets the history and culture of the African-American community of the nearby Sea Islands. The 1896 wooden cottage, which was transplanted to its present site on East Huntington Street, displays Victorian gingerbread detailing on the porch and dormers.

Driving and walking tours enable visitors to enjoy Savannah's architectural heritage. A visitor center, housed in the former Central of Georgia Railroad station, offers information on the city's historic districts.

FOR MORE INFORMATION:
Savannah Area Convention and Visitors Bureau, 222 West Oglethorpe Ave., Savannah, GA 31402-1628; 912-944-0456.

The Owens-Thomas House, below, is a Regency-style house with an inner courtyard.

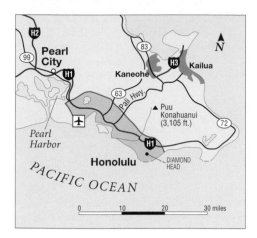

Waikiki Beach, Hawaiian for "spouting water," was named for the streams and springs that fed the marsh that once lay behind it. Waikiki attracts about 95,000 people each day, some 76,000 of whom are tourists who enjoy its boulevards, beaches, and ever-rolling surf.

T he port city of Honolulu is the only place in America where travelers can climb a dormant volcano, tour a royal palace, and test the surf at a beach fit for kings—all within a radius of a few miles.

The largest city in Hawaii fans out from the harbor waterfront, where the Hawaii Maritime Center rekindles the island's maritime past with displays from the cabins of luxury liners to the tattoo parlors of World War II. Docked outside the boathouse are the 1878 *Falls of Clyde*, reputed to be the last four-masted sailing clipper afloat, and the *Hokulea*, a replica of a traditional double-hulled sailing canoe. In 1976 this canoe drew the world's attention by making a successful 6,000-mile round-trip voyage to Tahiti, its crew relying solely on ancient navigational techniques.

ROYAL HISTORY

Honolulu is dotted with reminders that it was once home to Hawaii's royal rulers. The statue of King Kamehameha I in downtown Honolulu was dedicated in 1883. This sculpture of the king was financed with the insurance money from the original statue, which was lost at sea during its voyage from Paris, where it had been sculpted. Behind the statue stands Aliiolani Hale, ("House of Chief Unto Heavens"), commissioned in 1869 as a palace for Kamehameha V and redesigned as a state courthouse after Hawaii's monarchy was overthrown 24 years later.

Across the street, lush grounds surround Iolani Palace. Completed in 1882 as a residence for King Kalakaua, Hawaii's last monarch, the palace includes a throne room that displays the king's thrones and crowns and a royal kapu stick crafted from the tusk of a narwhal, an arctic cetacean. The widely traveled ruler equipped his palace with Honolulu's first telephone and installed electric lighting, making it the first electrified building in Hawaii.

The arrival of Christian missionaries had a profound effect on Hawaii, and numerous symbols of their presence remain in the city. One is the 1842 Kawaiahao Church, designed by Congregationalist minister Hiram Bingham; the church was constructed from 14,000 half-ton coral blocks quarried from offshore reefs by Hawaiian laborers. Nearby stands the Mission Houses Museum, which includes a kitchen where missionary women once learned to cook native foods. When the kitchen was in use, Hawaiian children watched in amazement through the windows, knowing that in Hawaiian tradition only men were allowed to prepare meals.

In order to facilitate the conversion of the islanders, missionaries devised a 12-letter Hawaiian alphabet to write biblical tracts and textbooks in Hawaiian. In the 1841 Printing Office visitors can see a replica of the wood-and-iron press used to publish these texts.

Founded in 1889, the Bishop Museum contains the world's largest collection of Hawaiian and Pacific artifacts, including brightly colored feathered garments worn by Hawaii's kings, heirlooms of the royal family, and ancient wood and stone effigies of various Hawaiian gods.

The two-mile strip of beach named Waikiki was once an amphitheater for the daring feats of Hawaii's surfing monarchs. Sunbathers can climb Diamond Head, a 760-foot-high volcanic crater at one end of the beach. Originally known as Laeahi ("Brow of the Tuna"), the peak was later renamed by a British sailor who mistook the crater's calcite crystals for diamonds.

Heading inland, visitors can see the crater of an extinct volcano, which holds the remains of nearly 25,000 men and women who perished during various wars while fighting for the United States. Dedicated in 1949, Punchbowl National Cemetery of the Pacific is studded with marble slabs and landscaped with monkey-pod and banyan trees. A view from the crater rim encompasses Diamond Head, Waikiki Beach, Pearl Harbor, and the State Capitol, completed in 1969 for more than $26 million. Designed by architect John Carl Warnecke, the building captures the essence of Hawaii with its volcanolike chambers, palm-shaped pillars, and reflecting pools that suggest the sea.

FOR MORE INFORMATION:
Hawaii Visitors Bureau, 2270 Kalakaua Ave., Suite 801, Honolulu, HI 96815; 808-923-1811.

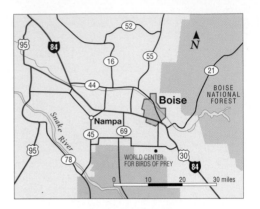

the Boise Greenbelt. With a population of about 150,000, Boise ranks among the fastest-growing cities in the nation.

Idaho's capital and largest city preserves its heritage in the Boise Historic District, which encompasses the 1892 Masonic Hall, 1879 Perrault Building, Spiegle Grocery (now Pengilly's Saloon), and the 1864 Cyrus Jacobs House, among other sites. The last building once served as a boarding-house for hundreds of Basque sheepherders who migrated to Boise from Spain in the late 1800's and early 1900's. Built by pio-

energy for residential heating. Its 1920 capitol is the only statehouse heated with this source of energy. Patterned after the nation's capitol, the building was cons-tructed of sandstone that was quarried by convicts from the nearby state penitentiary. The dome is graced with Corinthian columns and topped with a 250-pound eagle made of copper.

NEW TERRITORIAL CAPITAL

By 1864 the territorial governor had desig-nated Boise to replace Lewiston as the capi-tal. When Lewiston's townspeople balked at the loss, the governor stole the govern-ment's archives and seal from Lewiston and smuggled them to Boise.

After the 1860's gold rush was over and the miners left, Boise's population declined. Still, new construction and the expansion of irrigation in the valley kept Boise from becoming a ghost town. By 1887, when the Idaho Central Railroad linked Boise to the Oregon Short Line, the pioneer town was a hub of commerce and transportation for miners, farmers, and immigrants.

The valley attracted a bevy of criminals in those early days, and in 1870 a territorial prison was built in Boise. Its cells soon housed a motley array of horse thieves, rustlers, and other outlaws. Operating as a prison until 1974, the Old Idaho Penitentiary now displays contraband weapons and documents various escape attempts. Self-guided tours of the prison take in death row, the gallows, and cell houses—including "Siberia," the solitary-confinement block—and cells with one-way mirrors that allowed guards to make secret security checks. "Marked Men," an exhibit on prison tattoos, displays photographs of tattooed inmates and the equipment used for printing on skin.

Travelers can observe some of nature's predators at the World Center for Birds of Prey, located just south of town. Equipped with an incubator and laboratories, the center operates as a breeding facility for such raptors as hawks, falcons, and eagles. Young birds are hatched and nurtured here before being removed to release sites in the nearby Snake River Birds of Prey National Conservation Area, a 485,000-acre refuge harboring the greatest concentration of nesting raptors on the continent.

The 153-acre Ann Morrison Park, above, was funded by Harry Morrison, founder of the major construction-engineering company Morrison Knudsen Co., in memory of his wife.

The forested banks of the Boise River provided a shady haven for French-Canadian trappers, who journeyed across the territory's semiarid plain in the 1820's. They named the valley *Boisé,* a French word meaning "Wooded." Travelers on the Oregon Trail made frequent stops in the cottonwood-clad basin, but the trees offered little protection from the Shoshone-Bannock people. After a series of violent confrontations along the trail, the army built Fort Boise near the river in 1863. Stationed near a trail that linked the Boise and Owyhee gold-mining districts, the out-post guarded the region and allowed immi-grants to settle in the valley.

Today the City of Trees is a leafy oasis nestled in the sagebrush-covered slopes of the foothills of the Rocky Mountains. The placid waters of the Boise River course through town, fringed by a 19-mile-long paved bicycle and pedestrian path called

neer merchant Cyrus Jacobs, the brick structure is now part of the Idaho Basque Museum and Cultural Center.

From its original site near Cyrus Jacobs' home, the old adobe house of former mayor Thomas Logan was moved to the Idaho Historical Museum and Pioneer Village. Surrounded by 90-acre Julia Davis Park, the village also includes a frame house from the late 19th-century, a cabin built with pieces of driftwood, and a board-and-batten shack dating to 1909. Museum exhibits on Idaho history include those on cowboy culture, Native American life, and Idaho's Chinese gold miners. Other dis-plays re-create an 1800's kitchen, dining room, and parlor, as well as the A. C. Smith Saloon from the old Overland House hotel.

When Overland House hotel owner Hosea Eastman and his partners tapped the local hot springs in 1890, Boise became the first town in the nation to use geothermal

FOR MORE INFORMATION:

Boise Convention and Visitors Bureau, Visitor Center, 2739 Airport Way, Boise, ID 83705; 208-344-7777 or 800-635-5240.

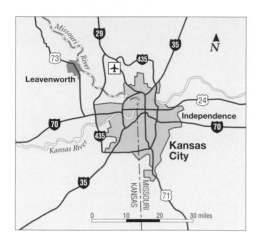

Kansas City, Missouri's distinctive skyline, above, reflects a blend of 1930's Art Deco–style high-rises with modern skyscrapers, the tallest of which is the 42-story One Kansas City Place.

For visitors expecting a Midwestern cow town, Kansas City comes as something of a surprise. It is said that only Rome has more fountains than this well-planned city of tree-lined boulevards and elegant architecture. Located where the Kansas River joins the Missouri River, Kansas City—K.C. to natives and visitors alike—is split between the states of Missouri and Kansas, with the border running along the aptly named State Line Road. The metropolitan area sprawls over seven counties in both states and incorporates its eastern neighbor, Independence, Missouri, a town forever associated with plain speaking Pres. Harry S. Truman, who lived much of his life there.

In the mid-1800's Kansas City and Independence were the springboard for homesteaders bound for the West. Because the Missouri was not navigable above this point, steamboats from St. Louis tied up here and emigrants then set off overland to join the California, Oregon, or Santa Fe trails. This period of K.C.'s history is recalled at the National Frontier Trails Center in Independence, where displays and interpretive exhibits include one of the covered wagons that rolled West.

Kansas City has a variety of exciting museums. The Nelson–Atkins Museum of Art houses nearly 30,000 items, including works by European old masters and such contemporary artists as Andy Warhol. The museum's 17-acre lawn is the site of the fanciful work of art called *Shuttlecocks*, sculpted by artists Claes Oldenburg and Coosje van Bruggen; its aluminum-and-fiberglass-reinforced plastic shuttlecocks rise 18 feet into the air.

The city's riverfront district is home to the Arabia Steamboat Museum, which offers a poignant snapshot of the frontier era. When the steamboat *Arabia* hit a tree snag and sank near Kansas City in 1856, it took with it a cargo of goods that was destined for the frontier. The museum displays 200 tons of items that were salvaged from the wreck in 1988. The booty includes clothing, tools, china, guns, medicine, whale-oil lamps, and bottled fruit.

Renowned for its fondness for barbecue, Kansas City has nearly 90 establishments purveying slow-smoked ribs, chicken, and fish. Every October more than 300 teams of barbecuers compete by presenting homemade sauces and ribs at the American Royal BBQ Contest, the largest in the world.

JAZZY CITY

The Kansas City Blues and Jazz Festival, held in July, attracts more than 125,000 visitors to K.C.'s Penn Valley Park. An essential stop for jazz fans is the 18th & Vine Historic District. In the 1930's the city's nightclubs, clustered around 18th and Vine streets, gave birth to a new brand of jazz, firmly rooted in the blues and expressed by such talents as Count Basie, Jay McShann, Andy Kirk, and K.C.-born Charlie "Yardbird" Parker. The museums at 18th and Vine include the 18th and Vine Visitors Center, the Jazz Hall of Fame, the Gem Theater, the Negro Leagues Baseball Museum, and the Black Archives of Mid-America, one of the nation's largest repositories of African-American art, painting, and sculpture.

FOR MORE INFORMATION:
Convention and Visitors Bureau of Greater Kansas City, 1100 Main St., Suite 2550, Kansas City, MO 64105-2195; 816-221-5242 or 800-767-7700.

The headquarters for the Pony Express operated from the 1856 Alexander Majors House, left, named for one of the founders of the Pony Express.

Wrought-iron balconies, left, are a typical feature of the French Quarter's 18th-century Spanish Colonial–style architecture.

Cradled in an interval between Lake Pontchartrain and the Mississippi River, New Orleans has survived just about everything—floods, fire, warfare, and the maneuvers of stubborn politicians. Established by the French in 1718, it became Spanish territory from 1763 to 1800. After fires damaged the city in 1788 and 1794, its Spanish rulers rebuilt its architecture in typical Colonial style—brick and stucco walls, tiled roofs, and delicate wrought-iron balconies.

The French Quarter, considered the heart of New Orleans, displays much of this Spanish-style architecture. Originally called the *Vieux Carré* (meaning "Old Quarter" in French), its basic grid was laid down by the founding French. Walking tours take in the 1792 Merieult House, which holds a fine collection of exhibits relating to the history of the city, and the 1831 Hermann-Grima House, one of the quarter's only examples of American Georgian–style houses. Walkers can also visit the district's

Napoleon House. The house was reputedly offered to the deposed French emperor, but Bonaparte died before his rescuers could free him from imprisonment on St. Helena. Now transformed into a bar, the house is one of New Orleans' coziest watering holes.

Jackson Square lies at the center of the French Quarter, presided over by a bronze equestrian statue of Andrew Jackson sculpted by American Daniel Clark Mill. Old Hickory is so honored because in 1815 he led a ragtag army against the British to win the Battle of New Orleans—the final battle of the War of 1812.

The triple steeples of the 1794 St. Louis Cathedral—the nation's oldest active cathedral—tower above Jackson Square. On one side of the cathedral stands the Cabildo, the old seat of the Spanish Colonial authorities; on the other is the Presbytere, built to house the cathedral's clergy, but now home to the Louisiana State Museum.

Uptown from the French Quarter is the Garden District, settled by Americans who came south after 1803, when the U.S. government purchased France's vast Louisiana Territory. Elegant, pillared Greek Revival homes sit amid gardens shaded by live oak trees shrouded in Spanish moss.

CITY OF MUSIC

New Orleans is synonymous with jazz, and Bourbon Street is forever linked to the music that emerged from the saloons, brothels, funerals, and street marches of turn-of-the-century New Orleans. The venerable Preservation Hall is a shrine to old-time Dixieland jazz. Today the city's biggest musical event is the annual New Orleans Jazz and Heritage Festival, held in early summer. Still, at any time of year New Orleans clubs are home to an amazing variety of music—rhythm and blues, Cajun, zydeco, contemporary jazz, and more.

The real highlight of the New Orleans calendar is, of course, Mardi Gras. Beginning on January 6 (Twelfth Night) and climaxing at midnight on Mardi Gras (Fat Tuesday, 46 days before Easter), the festival is a continuous bacchanal featuring lavish parades, costume balls, and innumerable parties. The merrymaking spills into the streets, and the French Quarter is closed to traffic. On Ash Wednesday the city returns to normal—until the following year.

FOR MORE INFORMATION:
New Orleans Metropolitan Convention and Visitors Bureau, 1520 Sugar Bowl Dr., New Orleans, LA 70112; 504-566-5011 or 800-672-6124.

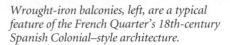

A St. Charles Avenue streetcar, left, clangs its way through the leafy Garden District. The streetcar, which runs on America's oldest continuously operating streetcar line, dates to 1835. One of the line's most famous streetcars starred in the 1951 movie A Streetcar Named Desire.

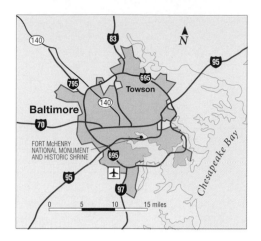

A city of firsts, Baltimore boasts the country's first railroad station and first cathedral, as well as the world's first telegraphic communications. The energetic spirit that fueled the growth from its founding in the 1660's remains an active force in modern Baltimore, where recent urban renewal projects have inspired the nickname Charm City and transformed Baltimore from a shell-shocked casualty of the 1960's and 1970's into one of America's most livable urban areas.

MARITIME ORIGINS

In the mid-1700's and early 1800's, Baltimore was renowned for its shipbuilders, who produced a generation of schooners known as Baltimore Clippers. Dozens of privateers commissioned the high-speed vessels, and by 1812, the city was the home port for 126 pirate ships.

During the War of 1812, the United States sent buccaneers from Baltimore to prey on enemy merchant ships. In response, the British vowed to obliterate the "nest of pirates" from Baltimore Harbor with a crack invasion force. The invasion fleet penetrated the harbor and bombarded Fort McHenry for 25 hours—but the fort and its men held firm.

Watching the battle all night from a nearby ship was an American lawyer named Francis Scott Key. The next morning, as the British withdrew, Key witnessed his compatriots hoist an enormous American flag in victory. He was so moved by the sight that he wrote a poem titled "The Star-Spangled Banner." Today a replica of the flag proudly flies over the ramparts of Fort McHenry, a star-shaped structure on the tip of Locust Point. (The original flag hangs in the Smithsonian Institution's Museum of American History in Washington, D.C.) A self-guided tour of the fort takes visitors through the barracks, officers' quarters, guardhouses, and the powder magazine.

Baltimore became a major transportation hub in the 19th century with the construction of westward toll roads and such engineering projects as the Chesapeake & Ohio Canal (linked to Baltimore by a spur canal) and the arrival of the Baltimore & Ohio Railroad in 1842. The B&O Railroad Museum preserves an extensive collection of vintage locomotives and reproductions, including a replica of America's first locomotive, the 1830 *Tom Thumb*. The 40-acre site encompasses the old Mount Clare Station, the country's first freight and passenger station, which now contains dioramas, bridge models, and a miniature railroad. A display of telephones and telegraph apparatuses honors inventor Samuel F. B. Morse, who transmitted the first telegraph message ("What hath God wrought?") from the station in 1844.

Although many Baltimore houses were destroyed by a fire in 1904, much of the city's history is preserved in monuments and museums scattered about town. The nation's oldest cathedral, the Basilica of the Assumption, still stands at Cathedral and Mulberry streets. It was planned by Bishop John Carroll (America's first Roman Catholic bishop) and dedicated in 1821. Designed by architect Benjamin Henry Latrobe, the cross-shaped building is fitted with stained-glass windows and bells that sound the Angelus thrice daily.

The Washington Monument, another survivor from the first half of the 19th century, was designed by Robert Mills, better known for having drawn plans for the Washington Monument in the nation's capital. (His plans were rejected by the builders and never used.) Completed in 1829, Baltimore's 178-foot-high column and statue is the first formal memorial erected to George Washington.

Visitors can learn more about the city's heritage by strolling along Museum Row, where several sites afford a look at the city's past. The 1808 Charles Carroll mansion was the winter home of one of the signers of the Declaration of Independence. The Courtyard Exhibition Center highlights Baltimore's history from the 1930's to the present day.

Although the city ranks as America's 13th-largest metropolis, Baltimore's many distinct neighborhoods—including Little

The China Sea Marine Trading Company, right, at Fells Point in Baltimore, is a marine supply company that was founded in 1980 and stocks a jumble of one-of-a-kind items, including ship's wheels, ship bells, portholes, and marlin spikes.

Italy, Little Lithuania, Union Square, and the old seaport neighborhood of Fells Point—give it a small-town atmosphere. Revitalized areas of the city include the Inner Harbor, where visitors can meander along a brick quay and browse through shops, cafés, and museums. The harbor's showpiece is the National Aquarium, which contains huge multistory tanks of dolphins, sharks, beluga whales, and other sea creatures. Among the aquarium's re-created habitats are a tropical rain forest, an Allegheny pond, and the largest Atlantic coral reef exhibition in the country.

The Baltimore Maritime Museum displays three historic relics: a floating lighthouse called *Chesapeake;* the U.S.S. *Torsk,* a World War II submarine; and the Coast Guard cutter U.S.S. *Taney,* the only ship to survive the 1942 Japanese attack on Pearl Harbor that still remains afloat.

FOR MORE INFORMATION:
Baltimore Area Visitors Center, 300 East Pratt St., Baltimore, MD 21202; 410-837-4636.

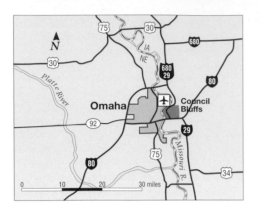

Union Station, above, the city's magnificent 1931 Art Deco rail terminal, houses the Western Heritage Museum. Among the items on exhibit here are a fully outfitted Conestoga wagon, historic documents, the Byron Reed Coin Collection, and restored railway cars.

Nebraska's largest city began life in the shadow of Council Bluffs, its neighbor and rival on the eastern bank of the Missouri River. In the early 1850's Council Bluffs was a thriving center for settlers and for fortune hunters bound for the California gold fields. Hungry for new opportunities, a group of merchants crossed the Missouri and set up a town on the western bank. From these modest beginnings, Omaha grew into the thriving city where more than 335,000 inhabitants live. Today it offers visitors a wealth of things to see and do.

Because of its position on the Missouri River, Omaha became an important transportation center. In 1863 Pres. Abraham Lincoln designated the town as the eastern terminus of the Union Pacific Railroad. The building of the railroad brought more jobs and settlers to the area. The Union Pacific Museum chronicles the railroad's role in opening the West through exhibits of model trains, surveying instruments, and paintings. Restored railcars are on display at the Western Heritage Museum, which interprets the history of Omaha from 1880 to the present.

Artistic works related to the opening of the West are displayed at the Joslyn Art Museum. Named for Omaha businessman George Joslyn and founded by his wife, Sarah, the museum displays paintings by artists Alfred Jacob Miller, George Catlin, and Frederic Remington, among others. One of the highlights is a series of watercolors depicting Native American peoples of the Upper Missouri, painted by Swiss artist Karl Bodmer in the 1830's.

With the settlement of Nebraska, Omaha became a prime location for the processing and shipment of agricultural produce. In 1883 a consortium of local businessmen formed the Union Stockyards Company in an attempt to turn Omaha into a livestock market that would rival that of Chicago. The gamble paid off, and the stockyards still represent one of Omaha's major industries.

A host of new arrivals of all races was drawn to booming Omaha in the late 1800's. The Great Plains Black Museum houses one of the most important collections of African-American historical material west of the Mississippi River. Omaha also preserves a site vital to the history of the Mormons' journey to Utah. In 1846 their leader Brigham Young secured permission from the U.S. government and the Omaha Indians to camp on the western bank of the Missouri. Some 3,500 Mormons camped here until they resumed their westward journey in the spring of 1848. The campsite came to be known as the Winter Quarters. Visitors can learn more about the Mormon legacy at the Mormon Trail Center in North Omaha.

BOYS TOWN
In 1936 on a farm near Omaha, a farsighted priest named Father Edward J. Flanagan set up a home for delinquent and homeless boys. The MGM motion picture *Boys Town* recounted the story of Father Flanagan's institution. Today more than 500 young people (girls have been admitted since 1979) live at Boys Town. Visitors can tour the Boys Town Hall of History and Father Flanagan's nearby residence.

The cold war is the focus of the Strategic Air Command Museum in Omaha, which tells the story of the strategic bomber forces that operated around the clock for 46 years.

From an underground command center at the Offutt Air Force Base—one of the air force's largest repair facilities—the men and women of the Strategic Air Command (SAC) controlled an arsenal of terrifying power. The museum displays a replica of this underground nerve center. Its collection of aircraft includes a B-29 Superfortress, built at Nebraska's Martin bomber plant, and the Lockheed SR-71 Blackbird, a high-altitude reconnaissance aircraft that can fly three times faster than the speed of sound.

With the redevelopment of its Old Market area, Omaha has successfully revived what was once a bustling produce market and warehouse district. Several turn-of-the-century Italianate buildings, including the 1887 Anheuser–Busch Beer Depot, were saved from the wrecking ball through the efforts of a group of local people. Today visitors can stroll the cobbled streets of this lively neighborhood and enjoy its wide range of specialty shops, restaurants, and art galleries.

FOR MORE INFORMATION:
Greater Omaha Convention and Visitors Bureau, 6800 Mercy Rd., Suite 202, Omaha, NE 68106-2627; 402-444-4660 or 800-332-1819.

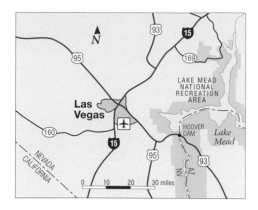

A roller coaster circles the top of the 1,149-foot tower of the Stratosphere Hotel and Casino, right, upholding Las Vegas' credo of entertainment at all costs.

Like a glittering mirage, Las Vegas rises abruptly from the bone-dry Mojave Desert of southern Nevada. For more than 50 years the city has been the symbol for hog-wild excess and the pursuit of pleasure. Nevada's liberal outlook on bootlegging, gambling, quick divorce, and prostitution guarantees the city a steady stream of tourists—more than 30 million a year.

Water has been key to the growth of the city. It was the presence of springs and creeks here that led Spanish explorers to confer the name *Las Vegas* (Spanish for "the Meadows") on the area. Nineteenth-century travelers along the Old Spanish Trail to California would stop here to rest and restock. The establishment of a railroad depot made it possible to bring in the heavy equipment needed to build the Hoover Dam on the Colorado River, 40 miles to the south. The completion of the dam in 1935 created Lake Mead, thus ensuring a virtually unlimited supply of water for the region.

The development of luxury casino-hotel resorts began with the construction of the Flamingo in 1946 by New York mobster Benjamin "Bugsy" Siegel. Gambling and organized crime went hand in hand until the late 1960's. More elaborate hotels, including the Sands, Desert Inn, and Caesar's Palace, have mushroomed along Las Vegas Boulevard and attracted their fair share of eccentrics. Billionaire Howard Hughes, for one, checked into the Desert Inn, laid down $13 million to buy the place, and didn't leave his suite for nine years.

The epicenter of downtown Las Vegas is the neon-lit Fremont Street—called Glitter Gulch—where casinos, hotels, clubs, and sideshows offer an eye-popping extravaganza of color. On Las Vegas Boulevard, various record-breakers are celebrated at the Guinness World of Records Museum. Nearby, the Imperial Palace Hotel houses the Imperial Palace Auto Collection, an assortment of more than 200 vintage automobiles that includes the bulletproof Mercedes used by Adolf Hitler.

Perhaps the most extravagant museum in the city is tucked away from the Strip on East Tropicana Avenue. Walter Valentino Liberace mesmerized audiences with his keyboard wizardry and his staggering ostrich feather suits, flowing fox and mink capes, and rhinestone-encrusted jackets.

At the Liberace Museum visitors can take a look at the flamboyant showman's glittery costumes, jewelry, customized automobiles, and pianos, including a piano played by Frédéric François Chopin and a concert grand owned by George Gershwin.

FAMILY ENTERTAINMENT

In recent years the city's formerly racy image has softened. Hotels now present shows ranging from medieval jousting tournaments to magic shows and replays of the sinking of the *Titanic*. Visitors can play the slot machines or roulette tables, take in a show, tour a museum, attend a boxing match, and zoom down the 76-foot-high slide at the 26-acre Wet'n Wild water theme park—all in the same day.

FOR MORE INFORMATION:

Las Vegas Convention and Visitors Authority, 3150 Paradise Rd., Las Vegas, NV 89109; 702-892-0711.

Since 1942 thousands of couples have recited their vows in the Little Church of the West, left, each year. The interior is made of redwood, reputedly from a single tree. The church is open daily from 8:00 a.m. until midnight.

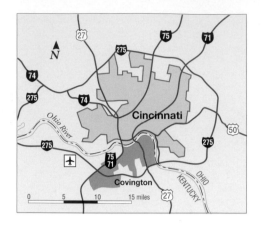

Although the Ohio River flats were first surveyed by three land speculators in 1788, it was not until the second decade of the 19th century that settlers began arriving by steamboat at the docks of the small village of Cincinnati in any significant numbers. In 1845 the Miami & Erie Canal opened and a steady stream of canal boats began to bring immigrants and supplies to the city. Houses mushroomed along the basin and soon moved up into the surrounding hills. For as long as rivers and canals were the principal routes for transporting both goods and people, Cincinnati ruled the Midwest.

After the Civil War, when the arrival of the railroads in the Midwest made river travel obsolete, Chicago gradually eclipsed Cincinnati as the principal city of the region. In time, Cincinnati built its own railroad—the Cincinnati Southern. As a result, major manufacturers, including Fleischmann's and Procter & Gamble, established enterprises here and ensured the continuing development of the city.

Two years after the end of the Civil War, the city celebrated the opening of the John A. Roebling suspension bridge, which spanned the Ohio River and linked Cincinnati with Covington, Kentucky. Although the bridge had been commissioned some 20 years earlier, war, litigation, and labor disputes delayed its construction. The 2,252-foot-long bridge, which was the longest span and the first suspension bridge of its day, served as the model for engineer John Roebling's famous Brooklyn Bridge in New York City.

Today Cincinnati, the third-largest metropolis in the state, is a renowned convention center and industrial hub. The town, once described by Winston Churchill as "the most beautiful of America's inland cities," boasts two universities and a vital downtown area studded with tourist attractions. A 22-block Skywalk system provides visitors with a walkway that makes it possi-

ble for them to explore the downtown area without having to battle traffic. The centerpiece of the square is the 1871 Tyler Davidson Memorial Fountain, topped by a 43-foot-high statue titled *Genius of Waters*.

Walking tours of the downtown district take in the 1893 Cincinnati City Hall, an imposing pink-granite Romanesque building on Plum Street. Like several of the city's landmark buildings, it was designed by Cincinnati architect Samuel Hannaford, whose work shaped the city during the Victorian era. Other buildings by Hannaford include Elm Street's Victorian Gothic–style Music Hall and Beaux Arts–style Memorial Hall, and the French Second Empire–style Cincinnatian Hotel at Sixth and Vine.

Some travelers to the city arrive by train at Cincinnati Union Terminal, an Art Deco treasure that also houses two museums. The first, the Cincinnati Museum of Natural History and Science, displays a replica of a limestone cavern, complete with underground waterfalls and a live bat colony. The highlight of the second museum, run by the Cincinnati Historical Society, is a re-creation of the city's riverfront in the 1850's.

Cincinnati earned its jocular nickname of Porkopolis after the city became the

world's largest pork-packing center in the mid-1800's. But the industry's reliance on Southern markets led to divided loyalties during the Civil War; conflicts over the slavery issue resulted in a race riot in 1829 and the destruction of an abolitionist press in 1836.

Slavery also was the subject of Harriet Beecher Stowe's famous novel, *Uncle Tom's Cabin*. The story was inspired by Stowe's father, Lyman Beecher, one of the organizers of Cincinnati's Underground Railroad network. Visitors to the Harriet Beecher Stowe House on Gilbert Avenue can see where the writer lived as a young woman and view exhibits on the Beecher family and the abolitionist movement.

BASEBALL PRESIDENT

William Howard Taft also grew up in Cincinnati. The William Howard Taft National Historic Site preserves the 1857 birthplace and boyhood home of the 27th president and 10th chief justice of the United States. Taft was famous for his large size (he weighed more than 300 pounds) and his love for baseball—so much so that he started the custom of the president throwing the first ball at the beginning of each major league baseball season. Taft's fascination for the sport probably was inspired by the organization of the Cincinnati Red Stockings in 1869, the country's first all-professional baseball club.

The private art collection of President Taft's half-brother, Charles Phelps Taft, and his wife, Anna Sinton, is showcased in the 1820 Federal-style Taft Museum on Pike Street. Collections here include Chinese porcelains, old masters, and French Renaissance enamels. The series of landscape murals is the work of 19th-century African-American artist Robert S. Duncanson, who lived and worked in Cincinnati. In Eden Park, the Cincinnati Art Museum displays everything from classical Nabataean sculpture to Andy Warhol's tribute to Pete Rose of the Cincinnati Reds.

FOR MORE INFORMATION:

Greater Cincinnati Convention and Visitors Bureau, 300 West Sixth St., Cincinnati, OH 45202-2361; 800-246-2987.

Artist Richard Haas' 1983 trompe l'oeil graces the north side of the 1923 Kroger Building at the corner of Vine Street and Central Parkway. The mural depicts Cincinnatus, the Roman citizen-soldier for whom the city was named.

The glass dome of Oklahoma's state capitol, above, is distinguished by the state seal. Portraits of such celebrated Oklahomans as Jim Thorpe and Will Rogers decorate the walls of the rotunda.

I n "Route 66," Nat King Cole sang that "Oklahoma City looks mighty pretty," and so it must have appeared to thirsty motorists traveling the fabled transcontinental highway from Chicago to Santa Monica. With the building of the interstate system in the 1950's, Route 66 was phased out, but Oklahoma City has been revitalized in the intervening 40 years. The northeast section of the city, home to the famed Oklahoma City Zoo, is now the site of the vast Omniplex, which includes the Omniplex Science Museum, the Air Space Museum, the Red Earth Indian Center, and the International Photography Hall of Fame. Across town, the new Civic Center and nearby Myriad Botanical Gardens have helped transform the downtown core.

NOTORIOUS BEGINNINGS

What is now a city was nothing more than a Santa Fe Railroad depot when federal authorities opened up a 2-million-acre parcel of land—known as the Unassigned Lands. At the time, the area called Oklahoma Territory had been officially ceded to relocated Indian tribes from all over the country. Nevertheless, many pioneers wanted to settle within the bound-

aries of the territory, and on March 2, 1889, Pres. Benjamin Harrison signed his name to legislation that officially opened up the territory to potential homesteaders. The land rush, sometimes referred to as "the greatest horse race in human history," began at noon on April 22, 1889, when about 50,000 people swarmed across the boundary line. Within a few hours, 10,000 homesteaders had staked claims around the Santa Fe depot, and Oklahoma City was born.

The 10-acre Harn Homestead and 1889er Museum preserves the farm of Judge Harn, who prosecuted illegal claim jumpers—known as Sooners. Harn's house is furnished in period style. The site includes a barn with a windmill, a restored one-room schoolhouse, and a four-acre working farm.

Oklahoma National Stockyards, founded in 1910, is today the world's largest stocker/feeder cattle market, with auctions held on Monday and Tuesday mornings. The surrounding neighborhood, known as Stockyards City, is a cowboy hangout with tack shops, boot- and hatmakers, and the oldest restaurant in Oklahoma City.

The National Cowboy Hall of Fame and Western Heritage Center has recently finished a $32 million expansion, tripling its size. Its three halls of fame salute Western movie stars, great Westerners, and rodeo performers; its art collection includes the work of artists Frederic Remington, Charles Russell, and Albert Bierstadt.

Each day visitors stop to lay flowers and wreaths at the site of the Alfred P. Murrah Federal Building, destroyed in the tragic 1995 bombing. The fence surrounding the empty lot has become an impromptu shrine to the 169 people who died there.

FOR MORE INFORMATION:
Greater Oklahoma City Chamber of Commerce, 123 Park Ave., Oklahoma City, OK 73102; 405-297-8900.

Architect I. M. Pei's Crystal Bridge, left, at the Myriad Botanical Gardens, is a 224-foot-long, 7-story-high glass tropical conservatory.

133

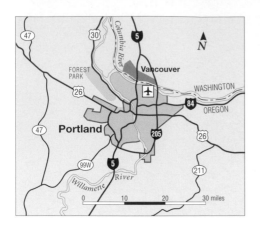

Framed by Portland's distinctive skyline, Mount Hood's snowy peak gleams white in February, above. With snow year-round, the mountain offers the longest ski season in the United States.

Blessed with idyllic scenery and a deepwater harbor, Portland straddles the banks of the Willamette River near its confluence with the Columbia River. Because no building rises more than 40 stories, Portlanders enjoy unobstructed views of Mount Hood, the snowy pyramid that towers 11,235 feet above Oregon's largest and most seductive city.

Portland's history began when a one-acre patch of the region's deep forest was cleared by the Chinook Indians, who cut trees for firewood. In 1843 Asa Lovejoy and Francis Pettygrove settled the clearing and flipped a coin to name the area. Pettygrove won the toss and christened the town Portland, after his hometown in Maine.

Portland's economy was bolstered early on by the supply of lumber and wheat to miners in California, Oregon, and Idaho. By 1851, the year Portland was incorporated, the city's population had reached 800, and its big-city status was confirmed with the arrival of the railroad in 1883.

Stone steps and azaleas, left, grace a hillside of the Japanese Garden in Washington Park. An authentic Japanese garden, the grounds contain a teahouse and a pavilion.

CITY OF GREEN SPACES

Portland is full of reminders of its storied past. The elm-shaded South Park Blocks contain the Portland Art Museum, where a collection of Northwest Coast Indian masks, textiles, and sacred objects is displayed. The Oregon History Center houses artifacts related to the city's past in a splendid museum, decorated with two trompe l'oeil murals by illusionist Richard Haas.

When the Pioneer Courthouse was built in 1869, it was so far from the town's center that residents joked about the need for the Pony Express to deliver the mail. Today the adjacent Pioneer Courthouse Square is paved with bricks inscribed with the names of the people who donated funds toward recent renovations of the square.

Today Portland has many green spaces, including the Grotto, a 62-acre park maintained as a spiritual shrine for all faiths. Crowned with a monastery, a massive cliff rises 10 stories up and around a grotto that serves as an outdoor cathedral.

Portland's favorite flower, the rose, is the centerpiece of two urban parks, including the Peninsula Rose Garden, one of the largest sunken rose gardens in America. At the International Rose Test Garden in Washington Park, visitors can stroll along paths edged with more than 500 varieties of the fragrant blooms. Elsewhere, water trickles through bamboo shoots in the Japanese Garden. The garden is laid out in five styles that typify Japanese landscaping.

Along with showcasing the natural beauty of the city, the parks are also home to architectural treasures. The Pittock Mansion, a sumptuous 22-room house built in 1914, is the showpiece of 4,700-acre Forest Park. The original owner, Henry Pittock, was the longtime publisher of *The Oregonian*, Portland's main newspaper. Designed in the French Renaissance style, the mansion offers breathtaking views of the Cascade Range and Portland's two rivers. Down by the harbor, the Old Town Historic District boasts one of the nation's largest concentrations of cast-iron building facades.

Michael Grave's Portland Building was the nation's first post-Modern public edifice. The office building has been likened to a birthday cake made of pink, blue, and cream concrete, and is decorated with *Portlandia*—a 36-foot-tall copper statue of a woman kneeling over a front door.

FOR MORE INFORMATION:

Portland Oregon Visitors Association, Three World Trade Center, 26 SW Salmon St., Portland, OR 97204-3299; 503-222-2223.

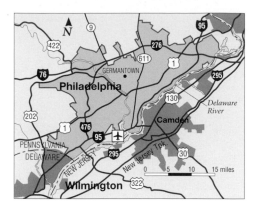

The summer sun dapples one of the buildings in Elfreth's Alley, right. Wedged between Second and Front streets in the historic district, this alley was where silversmith Philip Syng once lived. Syng made the inkstand used in the signing of the Declaration of Independence.

To walk the streets of Philadelphia is to tread some of the most historically significant ground in the entire nation. From its establishment in 1682, Philadelphia was a center of thought-provoking and radical ideas. Looking to build a society based on religious freedom and equality, Quaker leader William Penn took an undeveloped tract west of the Delaware River and laid out his "greene countrie towne" between what are now South and Vine streets. Penn called the settlement Philadelphia, Greek for "City of Brotherly Love." Quickly establishing itself as the pulse of the New World, Philadelphia was the scene of many of the dramatic events that led to the War for Independence, and was the place where leaders laid the groundwork for the philosophies and political system that still govern America today.

At the heart of the historic district—perhaps America's most historic square mile—visitors can see the hallowed halls where the nation's founding fathers once trod. Here, in Independence National Historical Park, stands a remarkable reconstruction of Declaration House, where 33-year-old Thomas Jefferson drafted the Declaration of Independence in 1776. In the handsome marble-trimmed Georgian building of Independence Hall, delegates from the Thirteen Colonies dissolved the union with Britain on July 4, 1776. The Liberty Bell Pavilion houses the famed 1753 bell that signaled the first public reading of the Declaration of Independence. Congress Hall was the seat of government and the place where George Washington and John Adams took their presidential oaths.

Other notable sites include the Betsy Ross House, Carpenters Hall, Free Quaker Meeting House, Old City Hall, Franklin Court, and the Colonial-style Christ Church, with its 200-foot-tall steeple.

The town's original residential district, Society Hill, was named after the long-defunct Free Society of Traders. Straddling the riverfront, Society Hill was the most valuable real estate in the city. Although the district later suffered years of neglect, approximately 800 houses have been restored since the 1950's, when urban renewal projects began to turn the area's fortunes around. Among the district's numerous architectural gems are the 1847 Athenaeum of Philadelphia, one of the city's first brownstone buildings; the Federal-style Hill–Physick–Keith House, built in 1786 and now open as a museum; and the magnificent Pennsylvania Hospital, founded in 1751 and the first hospital to open in the United States.

Washington Square, near Society Hill, served as a burial ground for Revolutionary War soldiers and victims of the yellow-fever epidemic of 1792. The shady park is the site of the Tomb of the Unknown Soldier of the American Revolution, a modest landmark bearing a statue of George Washington and the flags of the 13 original colonies.

FLEEING THE FEVER

Yellow-fever epidemics in the early 1790's killed more than 5,000 residents of Philadelphia, prompting the wealthy to retreat to summer estates in what is now Germantown. First settled by Germans in 1683, the bucolic countryside drew such notable figures as George Washington, who rented the 1772 Deshler-Morris House to escape the epidemic of 1793 and, having greatly enjoyed his stay, returned in 1794. The modest 1728 Stenton House of James Logan, William Penn's secretary, served as the model for the many Quaker-style country houses that grace the area. Germantown's Wyck House, one of the oldest houses still standing in Philadelphia, was owned by nine generations of the same Quaker family from 1690 to 1973, when it opened its doors to the public.

After America gained independence, Philadelphia served as the nation's capital from 1790 to 1800, when the government moved to Washington, D.C. During its brief reign as capital, Philadelphia was the largest city in the country. Not until 1810 did New York City command this title.

Nonetheless, Philadelphia remained the cultural center of the nation for some time. The Athens of America boasted such venerable institutions as the University of Pennsylvania, founded in 1740 by Benjamin Franklin and other prominent Philadelphians; the 1805 Museum of American Art of the Pennsylvania Academy of Fine Arts, the oldest art institution in the country; and the acoustically superb Academy of Music, a Renaissance Revival palace built for the Philadelphia Orchestra in 1857 and still in use.

Numerous other monuments and museums throughout the city are interspersed with modern condominiums and the towering descendants of the country's first modern skyscraper, the 32-story Philadelphia Saving Fund Society Building, which was completed in 1932.

Although the city suffers many of the ills that haunt urban areas, Philadelphia's well-preserved history and its status as one of the nation's most vibrant metropolises attests to the remarkable success of what William Penn called his "Holy Experiment."

FOR MORE INFORMATION:

Philadelphia Convention and Visitors Bureau, 1515 Market St., Suite 2020, Philadelphia, PA 19102; 215-636-1666.

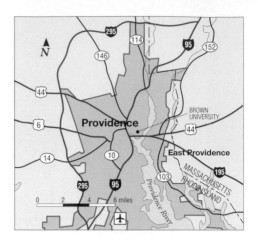

Robinson Hall, above, stands on the campus of Brown University. The seventh-oldest college in the country, Brown was established in 1764 under the name Rhode Island College.

The first permanent white settlement in Rhode Island was founded in 1636 by Roger Williams. A renegade preacher, he was banished from the Massachusetts Bay Colony for his radical pronouncements on religious freedom and his outspoken criticism of the royal charter that sanctioned taking control of Native American land by force.

Found guilty of promoting "newe and dangerous opinions against the authorities" in 1635, Williams escaped deportation back to England by leading his followers to an isolated site on the banks of what is now the Providence River. Here, Williams envisioned a colony where all people could enjoy religious freedom without fear of persecution. After purchasing land from the Narragansett Indians, he named the area Providence, meaning "Gift of God." Williams was soon joined at Providence Plantations by like-minded colonists, who cleared farmlands that quickly spread from the steep hills of the East Side to the tidal lands west of the river.

Agriculture remained Providence's primary source of income until the early 1700's, when its location and safe harbor made it an important stop along the New World shipping routes. Initially trading in rum and slaves from the West Indies and Africa, Providence's merchant class turned their sights—and ships—toward China following the War for Independence. The city was later the birthplace of the Industrial Revolution in New England, attracting a record number of immigrants from around the world.

BLENDING OF OLD AND NEW

A unique mixture of Old World tradition and modern innovation continues to set the pace of Rhode Island's capital. A microcosm of American architecture, Providence contains more Colonial and early Federal buildings than any other city in America.

The city's downtown is a masterpiece of urban renewal, accomplished by the removal of train tracks, the diversion of rivers, and the reestablishment of the historic Cove area as Waterplace Park. Edged with walkways, the four-acre park features boat landings, an amphitheater, a clock tower, and beautifully landscaped terraces.

A series of Venice-inspired bridges connects the downtown area with the historic East Side, where Roger Williams and his followers first settled along what are now North and South Main streets. A model of architectural preservation, the East Side is crowned by Capital Hill, the site of prestigious Brown University and the Rhode Island School of Design.

Benefit Street, often referred to as Providence's Mile of History, is one of 26 National Register Districts in the city. The mile-long thoroughfare and its side streets are dotted with brick mansions built with profits from the lucrative China trade.

Walking tours of the district are offered by the Providence Preservation Society, housed in the Shakespeare's Head building. Located at 21 Meeting Street, this edifice was erected by John Carter, the first postmaster of Providence and the publisher of the city's first paper.

The finest residence in the district is the 1786 John Brown House, built by merchant Joseph Brown for his brother, John. Design features include a bold Palladian window and a balustrade, which surrounds the roof. The 12-room mansion was described by John Quincy Adams as the most magnificent he had ever seen. The house is operated by the Rhode Island Historical Society.

Farther north stands the Providence Athenaeum, one of the nation's oldest libraries and cultural centers. Dating to 1838, the Greek Revival structure was the scene of Edgar Allan Poe's unsuccessful courtship of poet Sarah Helen Whitman.

Topped with a 185-foot steeple, the First Baptist Church was built in 1775. An exquisite Waterford chandelier, made in 1792, hangs from the ceiling. Founded by Roger Williams in 1638, this was the first Baptist congregation in America.

Elsewhere on Benefit Street, travelers can view the Old State House, a sober Georgian-style brick building erected in 1762. It was here, on May 4, 1776, that the colony's assembly passed an act that fulfilled Williams' desire for freedom by declaring Rhode Island the first free and independent republic in America.

The new state capitol, completed in 1904, stands on a hilltop west of the river. The New York architectural firm McKim, Mead & White used Georgia marble to construct the building; the dome is one of the largest marble domes in the world without a skeletal support. Paintings and relics adorn the interior of the capitol, including the original parchment charter of 1663 granted by King Charles II of England.

Back on the East Side, Roger Williams National Memorial Park surrounds the site where Williams discovered a natural spring and drank to "God's Providence." Exhibits and a brief slide show in the visitor center describe the life and works of this determined visionary, whose conviction that church and state should remain separate eventually was realized as law.

FOR MORE INFORMATION:

Providence/Warwick Convention and Visitors Bureau, One West Exchange St., Providence, RI 02903; 401-274-1636.

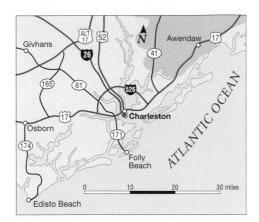

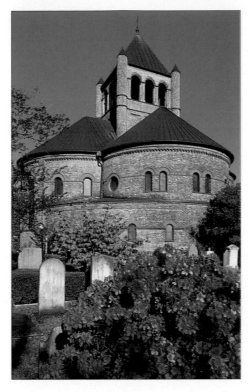

Named after King Charles II, Charles Town was founded across the Ashley River in 1670, and moved to its present site a decade later. Charleston, as it was incorporated in 1783, grew into a bustling seaport, prospering from local rice and indigo plantations and the slave trade.

The tenacious city survived the British occupation during the Revolutionary War and two years of bombardment by Union ships during the Civil War, only to be later plagued by disastrous fires, hurricanes, tornadoes, earthquakes, and financial hardship. Many of Charleston's buildings survived only because the impoverished residents were forced to repair damaged structures rather than build new ones.

Poverty had turned to pride by 1929, when the city became the first in the nation to zone a historic district. Today the city boasts some 2,000 heritage buildings, 136 of which date from the late 1700's.

Among the city's opulent mansions is the 1808 Nathaniel Russell House, built by a Rhode Island merchant for his family and their slaves. The sumptuous interior features a three-story, freestanding spiral staircase and numerous period antiques.

Located in the Battery (named for the fortified seawall), the Edmondston-Alston House is owned and partly occupied by descendants of the Alston rice-planting empire. Fronted with three-story piazzas, the Greek Revival edifice contains a library with nearly 2,000 leather-bound volumes.

The oldest of the city's many spires rises 186 feet from the base of St. Michael's Episcopal Church, built between 1752 and 1761. George Washington and Robert E. Lee both worshiped here.

A row of houses along Charleston's Battery District, right, displays the characteristic piazzas, or balconies, of the region. Houses were often staggered so as not to block the neighboring structure from cooling breezes.

The Circular Congregational Church, left, towers above the Charleston Cemetery—one of the oldest graveyards in the city.

A TASTE OF THE TROPICS

North of the Battery is an exuberant collection of Caribbean-inspired houses built in the mid 1700's and known as Rainbow Row. Painted in bright pastels, the buildings are typical of the style favored by merchants who lived above their shops.

Many outstanding examples of period furnishings are found in three historic mansions, which are owned and operated by the Charleston Museum. The Federal-style

Joseph Manigault House was designed in 1803 by architect Gabriel Manigault for his brother, Joseph. Reminiscent of a neoclassical villa, the mansion has a curving central staircase and the Gate Temple—based on Roman architectural design—in the garden.

Constructed in 1817, the Aiken-Rhett House is a Federal-style mansion with Greek Revival accents. Restored in the 1970's, its peeling Victorian wallpaper and tattered furnishings remain intact in rooms that were closed off for almost a century.

The Heyward-Washington House was built in 1772 by a rice planter named Daniel Heyward and was occupied by George Washington during a visit to the city in 1791. The austere brick facade reveals elegant interiors embellished with finely carved mahogany woodwork and rare Colonial furnishings, including an exquisite bookcase fashioned in 1770.

Some 13 blocks north of the Heyward-Washington House stands the Charleston Museum, which displays a world-renowned silver collection and fine examples of Charleston-made furniture.

FOR MORE INFORMATION:

Charleston Trident Convention and Visitors Bureau, P.O. Box 975, Charleston, SC 29402; 803-853-8000 or 800-868-8118.

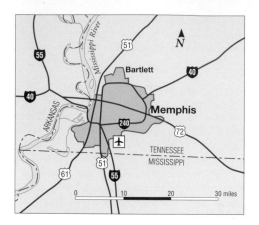

A number of antebellum structures are preserved in the Victorian Village Historic District, including the Italianate Mallory-Neely House, built around 1852. Continuous ownership by the Mallory-Neely family until 1969 left the interior remarkably intact; it features original stenciling on the ceilings, and wall coverings dating back to 1890. The front door is graced with a stained-glass window purchased in 1893 at the World's Columbian Exposition in Chicago.

Built in 1870, the nearby Woodruff-Fontaine House is trimmed with cypress

first blues song ever printed. The pulsating rhythm of the blues evolved in the honky-tonks of Beale Street, a predominantly black district frequented by the likes of Muddy Waters, Albert King, and Memphis-born Minnie McCoy.

Today the revitalized Beale Street Historic District is the vibrant hub of such Memphis nightlife and cultural institutions as the Center for Southern Folklore and the W. C. Handy Museum and Gallery, both containing exhibits on famous Memphians and the heritage of Southern music.

Memphis' most popular attraction is undoubtedly Graceland, the shrinelike mansion of the late King of Rock and Roll, Elvis Presley. Built in 1939, the 14-acre estate was purchased in 1957 by the 22-year-old singer for $100,000. Guided tours take visitors through Elvis' dining room, music room, den, and other rooms. The singer's army uniform and favorite Gibson guitar are housed in the Trophy Room, which displays Elvis memorabilia along with the star's collection of gold and platinum records and awards, representing 1 billion records sold. The tour ends with a visit to the Meditation Garden, where flowers adorn the grave sites of Elvis and other Presley family members.

The National Civil Rights Museum occupies the site where another celebrated American, Martin Luther King Jr., was assassinated in 1968. Exhibits and interactive displays focus on the history and seminal events of the civil rights movement and its leaders.

During the past three decades, urban renewal projects have earned Memphis such titles as the Cleanest City and Safest City in the Nation. Chief among the refurbishment projects was the establishment in 1982 of Mud Island Park, a 52-acre outdoor museum with exhibits on the Civil War, the Chucalissa Indians, and displays chronicling 10,000 years of river history. The island is home to the *Memphis Belle*—the first B-17 bomber to complete 25 missions in World War II without a casualty—and the river walk, a five-block-long scale model of the Mississippi River. Visitors can dip their toes into the flowing model, which details each bend, bridge, and major city along the river, tracing its snakelike course from Cairo, Illinois, to the Gulf of Mexico.

Shops along Beale Street, above, include numerous clubs and restaurants offering "good grub." Originally the home of the city's wealthy residents, the street, with its sometimes playful and eccentric character, is now the vibrant heart of Memphis.

Visitors to Memphis often describe it as a city of history and mystery. This is a nostalgic place, tied to its plantation past and enlivened by the mournful strains of the musical genre that originated here—a blend of slave ballads and Dixieland jazz known today as "the blues."

The riverside city was established in 1819 by entrepreneurs Andrew Jackson, John Overton, and James Winchester. Likening the Mississippi to the muddy waters of the Nile, the founders called the settlement *Memphis,* or "Place of Good Abode," after the city of the same name in Egypt.

By mid-century, Memphis claimed the world's largest inland cotton market, which was fueled by slave-driven plantations and a lucrative river trade. Bankers and brokers ruled the cotton kingdom, building opulent mansions to house their treasures.

wood and contains exhibits assembled from a 2,000-piece collection of Victorian clothing and accessories.

At the dawn of the Civil War, Memphis was a vital link in the Confederacy's supply chain. But in 1862, Federal gunboats sank a Confederate fleet and the town fell under Union control for the remainder of the war. Visitors to Confederate Park, on Front Street, can see the well-preserved Rebel ramparts used during the Battle of Memphis, as well as a statue of Confederate president Jefferson Davis, who resided in Memphis following the Civil War.

MEMPHIS MUSIC

The Memphis music scene didn't emerge until 1909, when trumpet player William C. Handy penned the notes of a song that was published as "Memphis Blues"—the

FOR MORE INFORMATION:
Visitor Information Center, 340 Beale St., Memphis, TN 38103; 901-543-5333.

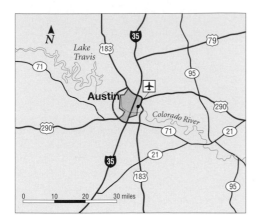

K nown as one of the leading universi-ty towns, pop-music centers, and high-tech meccas of the Southwest, Austin enjoys a rare mix of small-town charm and urban sophistication.

In 1837 the site on the edge of Comanche country was chosen for the pioneer village of Waterloo. Only one year later it was renamed for the Texas colonizer Stephen F. Austin and made the capital of Texas. The threat of Indian raids and the 1842 invasion by Mexican troops prompted Pres. Sam Houston to move the capital to Houston and later to Washington-on-the-Brazos. The government returned to Austin in 1844, however, and in 1850 it was declared the permanent capital of Texas.

In 1871 the isolated outpost was linked to the rest of the region with the arrival of the railroads, which facilitated the move-ment of goods and people. The subsequent founding of the University of Texas in 1883 attracted still more residents to the city.

THE CITY COMES OF AGE
The Bremond Block is one heritage site constructed during Austin's coming of age. A Victorian enclave, the block is com-posed of 10 magnificent residences built by two families connected by marriage, the Bremonds and Robinsons. Especially notable is the lacy ironwork and elaborate wraparound double gallery of the 1886 John Bremond Jr. House. The North-Evans Chateau was built in 1874 for Harvey North as a modest chateau and transformed into a Romanesque Revival castle when new wings were added to it by Maj. Ira H. Evans in 1894.

Austin's fourth state capitol is one of the largest in the country. Completed in 1888, the pink granite edifice is crowned

Located across the street from the state capitol, the Governor's Mansion, right, is typical of antebellum architecture.

with a pink metal dome that is seven feet taller than the capitol dome in Washington, D.C. The spacious interior features paint-ings, statues, and busts depicting the state's early years.

On the nearby University of Texas campus are located some of Austin's finest museums. These include the Texas Memorial Museum, which showcases research exhibits in sciences, and the Harry Ransom Humanities Research Center, which houses one of five extant Gutenberg Bibles. The Lyndon Baines Johnson Library and Museum honors the nation's 36th president with White House memorabilia and a library of 43 million documents associated with his presidency.

Beyond the university campus, the Congress Avenue and East Sixth Street District—once a skid row area— is now the vibrant hub of the Austin music scene. Restored Victorian and Renaissance Revival buildings, constructed of limestone and brick, are now occupied by restaurants, clubs, and live-music venues.

The most impressive building in the district is the 1886 Romanesque Driskill Hotel, built by Jesse Driskill, a cattle king and business tycoon. The brick-and-limestone exterior is studded with unusual carved stone accents, including busts of Driskill and his sons; a longhorn; and the Texas Lone Star.

In northeast Austin, central Texas' rural days are re-created at the Jourdan-Bachman Pioneer Farm, which maintains farm buildings from the 1880's. Costumed interpreters demonstrate such chores as cotton picking and syrup making as they portray the daily lives of three Texas fami-lies: the wealthy farmers who raised cotton

for the world market; the homesteaders from the Appalachian Mountains who worked the frontier; and the tenant farmers who endured the hardships of a sharecropping way of life.

FOR MORE INFORMATION:
Austin Convention and Visitors Bureau Information Center, 201 E. 2nd St., Austin, TX 78701; 512-478-0098.

The rotunda of the state capitol, below, is bathed in a golden light.

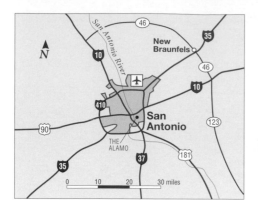

The River Walk, above, a two-and-a-half-mile pedestrian walkway, meanders along the banks of the San Antonio River. The area has a colorful mix of restaurants and nightclubs.

Known as the Cradle of Texas Liberty, San Antonio was originally the site of a Coahuiltecan Indian village. In 1718 Spanish settlers built the Franciscan mission of San Antonio de Valero here in an effort to convert the Native Americans to Christianity. The settlement was the capital of the Spanish province of Texas until it was captured by the Mexicans during the Mexican Revolution in 1821.

Renamed the Alamo in 1756, the mission was the scene of one of the most heroic chapters in Texas history. For 13 days in February and March 1836, 189 Texan volunteers led by William Travis, Davy Crockett, and Jim Bowie defended the Alamo from an onslaught by the army of Gen. Antonio López de Santa Anna of Mexico—an army that, by some estimates, numbered 5,000 men. Although the mission eventually fell, "Remember the Alamo!" became the rallying cry for Texans during their struggle for independence. Planted in the middle of downtown San Antonio, the Alamo site encompasses the restored limestone chapel and barracks.

MEMORABLE MISSIONS

While in San Antonio, visitors can tour four other well-preserved missions in the nearby San Antonio Missions National Historical Park. The missions San José, Concepción, Espada, and San Juan were built between 1720 and 1731 to help colonize the area. All four of the mission chapels are active Roman Catholic parishes serving the surrounding communities.

San José is regarded as the most spectacular mission. It encompasses several buildings and a chapel with an exquisite Baroque facade, considered one of the finest examples of stone carving in America.

One of the city's earliest residential settlements was established near the Alamo and today is known as *La Villita*, or Little Village. Here, cut-stone structures built by European immigrants are interspersed with earlier Spanish and Mexican stucco and adobe houses. Visitors can stroll along shaded cobblestone walkways and browse through art galleries, cafés, and craft shops.

Travelers can hop aboard a river cruiser on the San Antonio River for superb views of the city's arched bridges and riverside flora, including 75 species of trees, subtropical plants, and colorful flowers.

Early German settlers in San Antonio built elegant stone houses in the King William District. The Steves Homestead is a magnificent 1870's Second Empire residence with a slate-covered mansard roof and 13-inch-thick exterior walls made of limestone. The mansion contains a seven-piece parlor set, a Chickering piano, and a canopy bed where Robert E. Lee reputedly once slept.

German settlers are among the 27 ethnic groups highlighted in the Institute of Texan Cultures. Reconstructed dwellings representing rural Texas stand on the grounds. Inside, exhibits bring to life the customs, dress, and skills of the various groups who settled the Lone Star State.

The Arneson River Theater, left, is perched upon the banks of the San Antonio River. In the summer months, visitors watch Mexican folk-dancing from the grassy bank across the river.

FOR MORE INFORMATION:
San Antonio Convention and Visitors Bureau, 317 Alamo Plaza, San Antonio, TX 78205; 210-270-8748 or 800-447-3372.

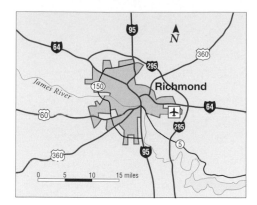

The capital of Virginia, Richmond, is situated on the James River. The area presently occupied by the city was first discovered in 1607 by a group of Englishmen. In 1644 Fort Charles was erected, and in 1733 the settlement was named Richmond, after a village in England.

A genteel city of the Old South, Richmond is studded with historic shrines commemorating the city's illustrious past. One is the 1741 St. John's Episcopal Church, the site of the Virginia Convention in 1741. Delegates included such prominent colonial figures as George Washington, Thomas Jefferson, and Patrick Henry.

A series of Union generals tried to capture the Southern capital during the Civil War, but the city was not taken until 1865, when Ulysses S. Grant's siege at Petersburg ended in the Confederacy's downfall. As Union troops advanced, Richmond citizens torched the wheat and tobacco warehouses to deny their revenue to the Yankees.

James H. Dooley, who helped revive the city's economy after the war, built his home beside the river in 1890, calling it Maymont. Surrounded by Victorian gardens, the 33-room Romanesque house features Rococo Revival interiors and remarkable furniture, including a table and chair with legs fashioned from narwhal tusks, and a bed shaped like a gigantic swan.

The Watt House, above, with its distinctive twin chimneys, is located in the Gaines' Mill Battlefield, which is part of the Richmond National Battlefield Park. On June 27, 1862, Robert E. Lee scored a decisive victory over Union forces at this site.

PERIOD OF REBUILDING

Postwar exuberance fueled the construction of the eccentric Old City Hall, designed by Elijah Myers and completed in 1894. An eclectic mélange of arches, gilded columns, and cone-shaped turrets, the edifice is graced with eye-catching interiors painted in exuberant colors.

Richmond's Court End is the site of the Valentine Museum, which contains exhibits of clothing, silver, and other period items. The adjacent Wickham-Valentine House is a 17-room Regency mansion filled with 19th-century furniture and a parlor painted with scenes from the *Iliad*.

Built in 1818, the White House of the Confederacy was occupied by Pres. Jefferson Davis during the war years of 1861 to 1865. The museum next door houses the world's largest collection of Confederate artifacts, including side arms, tattered uniforms, battle flags, and military documents.

A few blocks away, the John Marshall House was the residence of Richmond's leading citizen and the nation's chief justice from 1801 to 1835. Built in 1791, the brick Federal building contains Marshall family mementoes and furnishings.

Richmond suffered decades of neglect in the early 20th century, but a number of historic districts have since been restored. Among them is Shockoe Slip, a former commercial area along the river. The district's old warehouses have been renovated into apartments and condominiums, and its re-cobbled streets are now lined with craft shops and trendy boutiques.

FOR MORE INFORMATION:
Metro Richmond Convention and Visitors Bureau, 550 E. Marshall St., Richmond VA, 23219; 804-782-2777 or 888-742-4666.

INDEX

142

PICTURE CREDITS

ACKNOWLEDGMENTS

Cartography: Dimensions DPR, Inc.; map resource base courtesy of the USGS.

The editors would also like to thank the following: Lorraine Doré, Pascale Hueber, Bob Krist, Geneviève Meyer, and Valery Pigeon-Dumas.